Say It Right in

ARABIC

**Easily Pronounced
Language Systems, Inc.**

Clyde Peters, Author

New York   Chicago   San Francisco   Lisbon   London   Madrid   Mexico City
Milan   New Delhi   San Juan   Seoul   Singapore   Sydney   Toronto

The **McGraw·Hill** Companies

2 3 4 5 6 7 8 9 10 11 12 13 14 15 16   QFR/QFR   1 9 8 7 6 5 4 3 2 1

ISBN 978-0-07-154458-0
MHID   0-07-154458-5

Library of Congress Cataloging-in-Publication Data

Peters, Clyde (Clyde Elias)
       Say it right in Arabic / Easily Pronounced Language Systems; Clyde Peters, author.
              p.   cm. (Say it right)
       Includes index.
       ISBN 0-07-154458-5 (alk. paper)   978-0-07-154458-0 (alk. paper)
       1. Arabic language—Pronunciation.

PJ6121 .S246   2008
492.71'52—dc22   2008019274

Also available: *Say It Right in Brazilian Portuguese* • *Say It Right in Chinese* • *Say It Right in Chinese, Audio Edition* • *Say It Right in Dutch* • *Say It Right in French* • *Say It Right in French, Audio Edition* • *Say It Right in German* • *Say It Right in Greek* • *Say It Right in Italian* • *Say It Right in Italian, Audio Edition* • *Say It Right in Japanese* • *Say It Right in Korean* • *Say It Right in Russian* • *Say It Right in Spanish* • *Say It Right in Spanish, Audio Edition* • *Say It Right in Thai* • *Dígalo correctamente en inglés [Say It Right in English]*

Author: Clyde Peters
Illustrations: Luc Nisset
President, EPLS Corporation: Betty Chapman, www.isayitright.com
Senior Series Editor: Priscilla Leal Bailey
Egyptian Arabic Consultant: Ahmed Abu Heiba
Font Design: Mark Dodge

CONTENTS

INTRODUCTION

The SAY IT RIGHT FOREIGN
LANGUAGE PHRASE BOOK
SERIES has been developed
with the conviction that learning to
speak a foreign language should be fun and easy!

All SAY IT RIGHT phrase books feature the EPLS
Vowel Symbol System, a revolutionary phonetic
system that stresses consistency, clarity, and
above all, simplicity!

Since this unique phonetic system is used in all
SAY IT RIGHT phrase books, you only have to
learn the VOWEL SYMBOL SYSTEM ONCE!

The SAY IT RIGHT series uses the easiest phrases
possible for English speakers to pronounce and
is designed to reflect how foreign languages are
used by native speakers.

You will be amazed at how confidence in your
pronunciation leads to an eagerness to talk to
other people in their own language.

Whether you want to learn a new language for
travel, education, business, study, or personal
enrichment, SAY IT RIGHT phrase books offer a
simple and effective method of pronunciation and
communication.

PRONUNCIATION GUIDE

Most English speakers are familiar with the Middle East country of **Egypt**. This is how the correct pronunciation is represented in the EPLS Vowel Symbol System.

All Arabic vowel sounds are assigned a specific non-changing symbol. When these symbols are used in conjunction with consonants and read normally, pronunciation of even the most difficult foreign word becomes incredibly EASY!

On the following page are all the EPLS Vowel Symbols used in this book. They are EASY to LEARN since their sounds are familiar. Beneath each symbol are three English words which contain the sound of the symbol.

Practice pronouncing the words under each symbol until you mentally associate the correct vowel sound with the correct symbol. Most symbols are pronounced the way they look!

THE SAME BASIC SYMBOLS ARE USED IN ALL SAY IT RIGHT PHRASE BOOKS!

EPLS VOWEL SYMBOL SYSTEM

(A)	(EE)	(I)	(O)	(oo)
Ace	See	Ice	Oak	Cool
Bake	Feet	Kite	Cold	Pool
Safe	Meet	Pie	Sold	Too

(ă)	(ĕ)	(i)	(ah)	(ow)
Cat	Men	Win	Hot	Cow
Sad	Red	Sit	Dot	How
Hat	Bed	Give	Mop	Now

(ou)
Could
Would
Should

The Arabic language is spoken in more than twenty countries and classical Arabic is the most popular written form. Modern standard Arabic is the universal spoken language. This SAY IT RIGHT phrasebook uses colloquial Egyptian Arabic pronunciation because it is widely used and understood throughout the Arabic-speaking world.

EPLS ENHANCEMENTS

There are some very important sounds used in the Arabic language for which there is no exact equivalent in English. The following enhancements will help you to remember the different sounds. If possible have an Arabic-speaking person pronounce the Arabic examples shown below and try to duplicate these unique sounds.

( ) The **Ayn** ⑩N is part of the Arabic alphabet. It looks like this (ع). The Ayn is a very difficult
⒜ sound for non-Arabic speakers to emulate.
    It is a constricted or strangulated ⒜ sound.
⒜ In the Vowel Symbol System you will see a crescent mark before or after a symbol to help remind you.

▪ The **Hamza** H⒜M-Z⒜ is basically a glottal
    stop. If you are familiar with the Scottish
ˈⓐ language you have heard the word bottle
ⓐˈ where the two **t**'s actually become the sound
    of air being constricted in the throat. An example is like the pause between the end of the first words in each of these examples: **Uh uh** or **Oh oh** in the English language. In the Vowel Symbol System it is represented by a small vertical dash. Practice as much as possible as it is an integral sound in Arabic.

EPLS CONSONANTS

Most consonants like **T**, **D**, and **S** are straight-forward and pronounced like English letters. However, Arabic has sounds that have no English equivalents. The following pronunciation guide letters represent some unique Arabic sounds

B   Pronounce this **EPLS** letter like the rolled Spanish **r**.

GH Pronounce this **EPLS** letter like the French **r**. This sound is gutteral.

K   This **EPLS** letter represents a sound similar to the English K but slightly **darker**. Lower your jaw and pronounce the **k** in the back of your throat. Notice that when you say the English word **c**ondo you open your mouth wider to get the deeper **k** sound.

KH These two letters represent a soft **k** sound as in the Scottish word lo**ch**.

H   This **EPLS** letter represents the breathy sound made when you blow on your glasses to clean them.

T T In Arabic, the consonant sounds of **T,D,S**, and **Z**
D D can be pronounced in an emphatic manner. This
S S simply means that their sound is **darker** or thicker
Z Z sounding than you would hear in English. Notice that the EPLS letters in the second column of the example are slightly wider and thicker than the letters in the first column. This is a reminder to pronounced these letters far back in the throat.

ΛRABIC ALPHABET

bic alphabet is made up of 28 consonants
written from right to left. Letters change
form depending where they appear: e.g.,
ial, medial, initial, and isolated.

Final	Medial	Initial	Isolated		
ل	ل	ا	ا	'Alif	As in ⓐ/ⓐ/ⓘ/ⓔ
ـب	ـبـ	بـ	ب	B	As in **b**ed
ـت	ـتـ	تـ	ت	T	As in **t**ie
ـث	ـثـ	ثـ	ث	TH	Not used in Egyptian Arabic
ـج	ـجـ	جـ	ج	ZH	Like the s in mea**s**ure
ـح	ـحـ	حـ	ح	Ḥ	As in **h**ot (breathy)
ـخ	ـخـ	خـ	خ	KH	As in lo**ch**
ـد	ـد	د	د	D	As in **d**ay
ـذ	ـذ	ذ	ذ	Th	Not used in Egyptian Arabic
ـر	ـر	ر	ر	R	As in a Spanish **r**
ـز	ـز	ز	ز	Z	As in **z**ipper
ـس	ـسـ	سـ	س	S	As in **s**ee
ـش	ـشـ	شـ	ش	SH	As in **sh**e
ـص	ـصـ	صـ	ص	S	**Emphatic S**

x

Final	Medial	Initial	Isolated		
ض	ـضـ	ضـ	ض	D	Emphatic d
ط	ـطـ	طـ	ط	T	Emphatic t
ظ	ـظـ	ظـ	ظ	Z	Emphatic z
ع	ـعـ	عـ	ع	( )	'Ayn as in a pause
غ	ـغـ	غـ	غ	GH	As in a French r
ف	ـفـ	فـ	ف	F	As in fun
ق	ـقـ	قـ	ق	Ⓚ	As in condo
ك	ـكـ	كـ	ك	K	As in key
ل	ـلـ	لـ	ل	L	As in love
م	ـمـ	مـ	م	M	As in mom
ن	ـنـ	نـ	ن	N	As in noon
ه	ـهـ	هـ	ه	H	As in him
ـو	ـو	و	و	W/ⓞⓞ	As in win / cool
ـي	ـيـ	يـ	ي	Y/ⒺⒺ	As in yes / eat

'Alif is the first letter of the alphabet. It is the most common letter and can have several different pronunciations based on its position in a word and/or regional dialect. Short vowels in written Arabic are made by placing symbols above or below consonants. Long vowels ⓐ, ⓞⓞ, and ⒺⒺ are written within the body of words.

ABBREVIATIONS

In Arabic, there are differences related to masculine and feminine gender. As you will notice, there is usually a subtle change in the last syllable. For instance the word for happy is said one way if you are a man and another way if you are a woman speaking, Example (1). However, if you look at Example (2) you will notice the second word changes when you are speaking to a man or a woman.

You don't have to think too much about these differences because EPLS has distinguished them for you; e.g., (m) for masculine and (f) for feminine. Likewise, you will see (To a man) or (To a woman) in Example 2 below to help remind you that the phrase changes depending on whom you are speaking to. In some cases EPLS will tell you where it is important to use a phrase (man to man) or (woman to woman).

Example (1)   I'm happy.

(m) انا مبسـوط / (f) انا مبسـوطة

ã-Nah Mah'P-SooT (m)

ã-Nah Mah'P-SooT-ah (f)

Example (2)   Who is it?

مـيـن ده؟

MEEN Dah (To a man)

MEEN DEE (To a woman)

PRONUNCIATION TIPS

- Each pronunciation guide word is broken into syllables. Read each word slowly, one syllable at a time, increasing speed as you become more familiar with the system.

- In Arabic it is important to emphasize certain syllables. This mark (´) **over** the syllable reminds you to STRESS that syllable.

- The pronunciation choices in this book were chosen for their simplicity and effectiveness

- To perfect your Arabic accent you must listen closely to Arabic speakers and adjust your speech accordingly. Don't forget to practice!

- All of the phrases in this book are written in simplifed Modern Standard Arabic script so if necessary you can just point to the phrase.

- The EPLS transliteration is in Colloquial Egyptian Arabic, which is spoken and understood widely.

- In Arabic, short vowels in written Arabic are made by placing diacritics and various symbols above or below consonants. Long vowels ⓐ, ⓞⓞ, and ⓔⓔ are written within the body of words. Additionally, Arabic script is written from right to left.

ICONS USED IN THIS BOOK

 ## KEY WORDS

You will find this icon at the beginning of chapters indicating key words relating to chapter content. These are important words to become familiar with.

 ## PHRASEMAKER

The Phrasemaker icon provides the traveler with a choice of phrases that allows the user to make his or her own sentences.

Say It Right in
ARABIC

ESSENTIAL WORDS AND PHRASES

Here are some basic words and phrases that will help you express your needs and feelings in **Arabic**.

Hello

اهلا

•@h-L@N

Lit: Family

Hi / Welcome

اهلا و سهلا

•@h-L@N W@h S@h-L@N

How are you?

ازايك؟

①-Z①-Y@K (To a man)

①-Z①-Y①K (To a woman)

Fine, thanks be to God

انا كويس/ كويسة الحمد لله

KW①-Y①S ①L-Ḧ@M-D⊚ L①L-Lĕ (m)

KW①-Y①-S@h ①L-Ḧ@M-D⊚ L①L-Lĕ (f)

Good morning

صباح الخير

SĀ-BaħH ĪL-KHĒʼR

SĀ-BaħH ĪN-NOŌʼR (Traditional response)

Good afternoon / evening

مساء الخير

MĪ-SĒʼ ĪL-KHĒʼR

MĪ-SĒʼ ĪN-NOŌʼR (Traditional response)

Good night

تصبح علي خير

TĪS-BaħH (Āʼ-Laħ KHĒʼR (To a man)

TĪS-BaħH-EE (Āʼ-Laħ KHĒʼR (To a woman)

TĪS-BaħH-OO (Āʼ-Laħ KHĒʼR (To a group)

Good-bye

مع السلامة

Maħ (ĀʼS-Saħ-LĒʼ-Maħ

Peace

سلام

SĀ-LĀʼM

Yes	No
ايوة	لا
·Ⓘ-Wⓐⓗ	Lⓐ·

Please

من فضلك

MⓘN Fⓐ̈D-LⓐⓗK (To a man)

MⓘN Fⓐ̈D-LⓘK (To a woman)

Note that these are pronounced differently depending on whether you are speaking to a man or a woman.

Thank you	You're welcome
شكرا	عفوا
SHⓞⓤK-RⓐⓗN	(ⓐⓗF-WⓐⓗN

Excuse me	I'm sorry
اسمح لي	آسف
ⓘS-Mⓐ̈Ḧ-LⒺⒺ	ⓐ̈-SⓘF

Mr.	Mrs.
السّيد	السّيدة
ⓘS-Sⓘ́-YⓘD	ⓘS-Sⓘ-Yⓘ́-Dⓐⓗ

Miss

الآنسة

ⓘL-·ⓐ̈-NⓘS-Sⓐⓗ

I understand.

انا فاهم / انا فاهمة

@-N@h F@́-H@M (m)

@-N@h F@́H-M@h (f)

I don't understand!

انا مش فاهم / انا فاهمة

@-N@h M@SH F@́-H@M (m)

@-N@h M@SH F@́H-M@h (f)

Do you understand?

فهمت / فهمتى؟

F@-H@́MT (To a man)

F@-H@́M-T@ (To a woman)

Do you speak English?

بتتكلم انجليزي؟   (To a man)

B@-T@T-K@́L-L@M ·@N-G@-L@́-Z@

(To a woman)

B@-T@T-K@́L-L@́-M@ ·@N-G@-L@́-Z@

Please repeat

من فضلك عيد كلامك
                                      (To a man)

M@N F@́D-L@K @́-@́D K@-L@́@-M@K

(To a woman)

M@N F@́D-L@K @́-@́-D@ K@-L@́@-M@K

FEELINGS

I would like… / I want...

انا عاوز / انا عاوزة

ⓐ-Nⓐⓗ (ⓘ-Wⓘz... (m)

ⓐ-Nⓐⓗ (ⓞⓦ-zⓐⓗ... (f)

I need…

انا محتاج / انا محتاجة

ⓐ-Nⓐⓗ Mⓐᴴ-TⓔG... (m)

ⓐ-Nⓐⓗ Mⓐᴴ-Tⓔ-Gⓐⓗ... (f)

I'm happy.

انا مبسوط / انا مبسوطة

ⓐ-Nⓐⓗ MⓐⓗP-SⓞⓞT (m)

ⓐ-Nⓐⓗ MⓐⓗP-SⓞⓞT-ⓐⓗ (f)

I'm sad.

انا حزين / انا حزينة

ⓐ-Nⓐⓗ Ḧⓐ-ZᴇᴇN... (m)

ⓐ-Nⓐⓗ Ḧⓐ-ZᴇᴇN-ⓐⓗ... (f)

I'm hungry.

انا جعان / انا جعانة

ⓐ-Nⓐⓗ Gⓘ-ⓐN (m)

ⓐ-Nⓐⓗ Gⓘ-ⓐN-ⓐⓗ (f)

I'm thirsty.

انا عطشان / عطشانة

ⓐ-Nⓐⓗ (ⓐⓗT-SHⓐⓗN (m)

ⓐ-Nⓐⓗ (ⓐⓗT-SHⓐⓗN-ⓐⓗ (f)

I'm tired.

انا تعبان / تعبانة

ⓐ-Nⓐⓗ Tⓐⓗ)-BⓔⓗN (m)

ⓐ-Nⓐⓗ Tⓐⓗ)-BⓔⓗN-ⓐⓗ (f)

I'm lost.

انا تايه / تايهة

ⓐ-Nⓐⓗ Tⓔⓗ-YⓔⓗH (m)

ⓐ-Nⓐⓗ Tⓘ-ⒺⒺ-Hⓐⓗ (f)

I'm in a hurry.

انا مستعجل / مستعجلة

ⓐ-Nⓐⓗ MⓘS-Tⓐⓗ)-GⓘL (m)

ⓐ-Nⓐⓗ MⓘS-Tⓐⓗ)-GⓘL-ⓐⓗ (f)

I'm sick / ill.

انا عيان / عيانة

ⓐ-Nⓐⓗ (ⓐⓗ-YⓘN (m)

ⓐ-Nⓐⓗ (ⓐⓗ-YⓔⓗN-ⓤⓗ (f)

Notice the subtle differences in pronunciation that are used depending on whether a man or woman is speaking about himself or herself.

INTRODUCTIONS

Use the following phrases when meeting someone for the first time both privately and in business.

My name is...

انا اسمي

ⓐ-Nⓐⓗ ①'S-Mⓔⓔ...

What's your name?

اسمك ايه؟

·①'S-MⓐⓀ ·Ⓐ (To a man)

·①'S-M①-Ⓚⓔⓔ ·Ⓐ (To a woman)

Pleased to meet you.

اتشرف

·①T-SHⓐⒷ-Ⓡⓐ'F-Nⓐⓗ

GENERAL GUIDELINES

Egypt is a Middle Eastern country deeply religious and characterized by Middle Eastern customs. Many museums, monuments, and cultural tourist sites are open between 9:00 AM and 5:00 PM daily. When visiting mosques, mausoleums, or madrasas you must remove your shoes. At these tourist destinations canvas overshoes are provided. It is advisable for women to cover bare arms and to wear a hat.

- Generally, most Egyptians will be happy to help you with your questions as they usually speak more than one language.

- It is important to note that Egyptians will stand closer than Westerners are accustomed to.

- You will usually be greeted with a smile and inquiries as to your health.

COMMON GREETINGS

When you are at a loss for words but have the feeling you should say something, try one of these! It's important to remember that religion is an everyday part of life in the Middle East and is a part of most greetings and common sayings.

God willing.

إن شاء الله

Ⓘ´N-SHⓐⓗ· ·ⓐⓗL-Ⓛⓐⓗ´

This is one of the most common phrases you will hear!

In the name of God.

بسم الله

Bⓘ´S-MⒾ-Ⓛⓔ

Often said before eating, drinking, driving etc.

Thanks be to God.

الحمد لله

Ⓔⓛ ĤⓐⓗM-DⓄⓄ LⓘⓁⓔ

Good luck!

بالتوفيق

BI-TOW-FEE·

Peace be with you.

السلام عليكم

aS-Sa-Lah-Moo (a-LA-KoM

And with you be peace.

و عليكم السلام

Wa (a-LA-KoM aS-Sa-LaM

Welcome

مرحبا

MaB-Hah-BaN

This is common in countries such as Jordan, Kuwait and Saudi Arabia.

Hello

كيف حالك؟

KAF HI-LaK

This is common in countries such as Syria, Lebanon, Palestine, and Jordan.

THE BIG QUESTIONS

Who?

مين

M**EE**N

Who is it?

مين ده؟

M**EE**N D**ah**   (To a man)

M**EE**N D**EE**   (To a woman)

What?

ايه؟

A

When?

امته؟

EM-T**ah**

Where? (is/are)

فين.

F⊛N...

Which?

انهي؟

·⊛N-H⊕

Why?

ليه

L⊛

How?

ازاي؟

⊙Z-Z⊛

How much? (money)

بكام؟

B⊙-K⊛M

How long? (time)

اد ايه؟

·⊛D ·⊛

ASKING FOR THINGS

The following phrases are valuable for directions, food, help, etc.

I would like… / I want…

انا عاوز / انا عاوزة...

ⓐ-Nⓐ (Ⓘ-WⒾ Z… (m)

ⓐ-Nⓐ (ⓞⓦ-Zⓐ… (f)

I need…

انا محتاج / انا محتاجة... ب

ⓐ-Nⓐ Mⓐﾄ-Tⓔ G… (m)

ⓐ-Nⓐ Mⓐﾄ-Tⓔ-Gⓐ… (f)

Can you? / Are you able to…? / May I ask…?

...ممكن

MⓞⓦM-KⓘN…

Always remember to say thank you!

Thank you

شكرا

SHⓞⓦK-RⓐN

PHRASEMAKER

I would like…

انا عاوز / انا عاوزة

ⓐ-Nⓐⓗ (ⓘ-WⓘZ… (m)

ⓐ-Nⓐⓗ (ⓞⓦ-Zⓐⓗ… (f)

▸ **coffee**   **more coffee**

   قهوة   قهوة كمان

ˈⓐ-Wⓐ   ˈⓐⓗ-Wⓐ Kⓐ-Mⓐ́N

▸ **some water**

   شوية مية

SHWⓘ Mⓘ́-Yⓐⓗ

▸ **some ice**

   شوية تلج

SHWⓘ Tⓐ́LG

▸ **the menu**

   القايمة

ⓔ́L Kⓘ́-Mⓐⓗ

PHRASEMAKER

Here are a few sentences
you can use when you feel
the urge to say **I need**... or **can you**...?

I need...

... انا محتاج / انا محتاجة

ⓐ-Nⓐⓗ Mⓐ́Ḧ-Tⓔ̆G... (m)

ⓐ́-Nⓐⓗ Mⓐ́Ḧ-Tⓔ̆-Gⓐⓗ... (f)

▶ **more money**

فلوس اكتر

FL◎◎S ⓐⓗK-TⓐⓗB

▶ **change** (money)

فكة

Fⓐ́K-Kⓐⓗ

▶ **your help**

مساعدتك

M◎◎S-Sⓐⓗ)-Ðⓘ-Tⓔ́K

▶ **a doctor**   ▶ **a lawyer**

دكتور / دكتورة   محامي / محامية

D◎◎K-Tⓞ́B (m)   Mⓞ-Ḧⓘ-MⓔⒺ

D◎◎K-Tⓞ́-Bⓐⓗ (f)

PHRASEMAKER

Can you...

ممكن...

M@M-K@N...

▶ **help me?**

تساعدني / تساعديني ؟

T@-S@h-@D-N@ (m)

T@-S@h)-D@-N@ (f)

▶ **give me...?**

تديني؟

T@-D@-N@ (m)

T@-D@-N@ (f)

▶ **tell me...?**

تقوللي؟

T@-@-L@ (m)

T@-@-L@-L@ (f)

▶ **take me to...?**

.توديني لـ؟

T@-@-D@-N@ L@... (m)

T@-@-D@-N@ L@... (f)

ASKING THE WAY

No matter how independent you are, sooner or later you'll probably have to ask for directions.

Where is...?

فين...؟

F@N...

I'm looking for...

.انا بدور على

@-N@h B@h-D@w-W@nB (@h-L@h...

Is it near?

ده قريب؟

D@h ①-B①-Y①B

Is it far?

ده بعيد؟

D@h B①-@D

I'm lost.

انا تايه / تايهة

@-N@h T@-Y@H (m)

@-N@h T①-@-H@h (f)

PHRASEMAKER

Where is...

فين...؟

F⊕N...

▶ **the restroom?**

التواليت؟

①T-TW⊕-L①T

▶ **the telephone?**

التليفون؟

⊕L T⊕-L⊕-FO'N

▶ **the beach?**

الشّاطى؟

⊕SH SH⊕-T① ·

▶ **the hotel?**

الفندق

⊕L FO'N-D⊚ ·

▶ **the train for...?**

القطر لـ... ؟

⊕L ·⊕TR...

TIME

What time is it?

الساعة كام؟

ⓘS-Sⓔ-⒜ K⒜M

Morning

الصبح

ⓘS-SⓄⓊBH

Noon

الظهر

ⓘD-DⓄHⱤ

Night

ليل

LⒶL

Today

النهاردة

ⓘNⓐH-HⓐⱤ-Dⓐ

Tomorrow

بكرة

BⓊK-Ɽⓐ

This week

الاسبوع ده

ⓔL ·ⓘS-Bⓞⓞⓐⓗ)-Dⓐⓗ

This month

الشهر ده

ⓔSH SHⓐⓗ-Rⓘ-Dⓐⓗ

This year

السنه ده

ⓔSH Sⓔ-Nⓔ-Dⓔⓔ

Now

دلوقتي

DⓔL-Wⓐⓗ-Tⓔⓔ

Soon

عن قريب

(ⓐⓗN ·ⓔ-RⓔⓔB

Later

بعدين

Bⓐⓗ)-Dⓐ́N

Never

أبدا

ⓐ́-Bⓐⓗ-DⓐⓗN

WHO IS IT?

I

انا

Ⓐ́-Nⓐⱨ

You

أنت

Ⓘ́N-Tⓐⱨ (m)

Ⓘ́N-TⒺⒺ (f)

You (plural)

انتم

Ⓘ́N-TⓞⓤM

He   **She**

هوه   هيه

HⓄ́-Wⓐⱨ (m)   HⒶ́-Yⓐⱨ (f)

We (are)

احنه

Ⓔ́H-Nⓐⱨ

THIS AND THAT

The equivalents of **this, that,** and **these** are as follows:

This

ده

D@h

This is mine.

ده بتاعي / دي بتاعتي

D@h B①-T@'-① (m) / D€€ B①-T@h-T€€ (f)

That

ده

D@h

That is mine.

ده بتاعي / دي بتاعتي

D@h B①-T@'-① (m) / D€€ B①-T@h)-T€€ (f)

These

دول

D∞L

These are mine.

دول بتوعي

D∞L B①-T∞'-①

USEFUL OPPOSITES

Near	**Far**
قريب	بعيد
ⓞⓞ-B①-Y①B	B①-ⒺⒺD
Here	**There**
هنا	هناك
HⓔҢ-Nⓐⓗ	Hⓔ-NⓐҚ
Left	**Right**
شمال	يمين
SH①-Mⓐ̈L	Y①-MⒺⒺN
A little	**A lot**
شوية	كتير
SHⓄ-①́-Yⓔ̈	K①-TⒺⒺR
More	**Less**
اكتر	أقل
ⓐҢK-TⓐⓗR	ⓔ-ⓐ̈L
Big	**Small**
كبير	صغير
Kⓔ̈-BⒺⒺR	SⓄ-GH①-YⓐⓗR

Open	**Closed**
مفتوح	مقفول
MⓐF-TⓄⓗ	Mⓐ·-FⓄL
Cheap	**Expensive**
رخيص	غالي
Bⓐ-ⓀⒽEE'S	GHⒺ-LⒺ
Dirty	**Clean**
موسخ	نضيف
MWⓐ-SⓐⓀⒽ	NⓄ-DⒺF
Good	**Bad**
كويس	وحش
KWⓄ-YⓄS	Wⓐ-ⒽⓄSH
Vacant	**Occupied**
فاضي	مشغول
Fⓐ-DⒺ	MⓐSH-GⓄL
Right	**Wrong**
صح	غلط
SⓐⒽ	GHⓐ-LⓐT

WORDS OF ENDEARMENT

I love you.

انا بحبك / انا بحبك

ⓐ-Nⓐ Bⓐ-Hˉⓔ-BⓘK   (Man to a woman)

ⓐ-Nⓐ Bⓐ-Hˉⓔ-BⓐK   (Woman to a man)

I like Egypt.

انا بحب مصر

ⓐ-Nⓐ Bⓐ-HˉⓔB MⓐSₐ

I like Egyptian food.

انا بحب الأكل المصري

ⓐ-Nⓐ Bⓐ-HˉⓔB ⓘL-ⓐKL
ⓘL-Mⓐ'S-Rⓔⓔ

WORDS OF ANGER

What do you want?

عايز ايه؟

(Ⓘ́Z Ⓐ

Leave me alone!

سبني في حالي

SⒾ́B-NⒺⒺ FⒶⒽ-Ⓗ́ⒶⒽ́-LⒺⒺ

Go away!

امشي

Ⓐ́M-SHⒺⒺ

Stop bothering me!

بطل مضايقة

BⒶ́T-TⒶL MⓄⓤ-DⒾ́-·Ⓐ́

USEFUL COMMANDS

Stop!

اقف

(O)-·(ah)F

Go!

روح

B(oo)H

Wait!

إستنه

(e)S-T(ah)N-N(ah)

Hurry!

بسرعة

B(oo)-S(O)R-(ah)

Slow down!

بالراحة

B(i)R-R(ah)-H(ah)

Come!

تعالي

T(ah)-(ä)-L(ah)

EMERGENCIES

Fire!

نار

Nⓐᴮ

Help!

الحقوني

ⒾL-Ĥⓐʰ´-·⑩-Nᴱᴱ

Emergency!

طوارئ

Tⓐʰ-Wⓐʰ-Ⓡⓘ·

Call the police!

اطلب البوليس

ⓐ´T-LⓄB ⓔL PⓄ-Lᴱᴱˢ

Call the doctor!

اطلب الدكتور

ⓐ´T-LⓄB ⓔL DⓞⓤK-TⓄᴮ

Call an ambulance!

اطلبْ / اطلبى الإسعاف

ⓔ´T-LⓄ´B ⓔL ⓔ´S-SⓘⰯⓔF (To a man)

ⓔ´T-LⓄ´-Bᴱᴱ ⓔL ⓔ´S-SⓘⰯⓔF (To a woman)

ARRIVAL

Passing through customs should be easy since there are usually agents available who speak English. You may be asked how long you intend to stay and if you have anything to declare.

- Have your passport ready.

- Be sure all documents are up-to-date.

- While in Egypt, it is wise to keep receipts for everything you buy.

- It is important to list items like cameras and computers that you are bringing into the country so that there isn't any trouble taking them back out of the country.

- Be aware that many countries will charge a departure tax when you leave. Your travel agent should be able to find out if this affects you.

- If you have connecting flights, be sure to reconfirm them in advance.

- Make sure your luggage is clearly marked inside and out and always keep an eye on it when in public places.

- Take valuables and medicines in carry-on bags.

KEY WORDS

Baggage

الشنط

SHŌ-NⓐⓗT

Documents

الاوراق

ⓔL (ⓞ̃ⓦ-Rⓐ̃·

Passport

الباسبور / جواز سفر

BⓐⓗS-Bⓞ́B / Gⓐ̃-Wⓐ̃Z Sⓐⓗ-FⓐⓗB

Porter

شيال

SHⓐ̃-Yⓔ́L

Customs

الجمارك

Gⓐⓗ-Mⓔ́-Bⓘ́K

Taxi

تاكسي

Tⓐ̃K-Sⓔⓔ

USEFUL PHRASES

Here is my passport.

ده جواز سفري

DⒶ Gⓐⓗ-WⒶZ Sⓐⓗ-Fⓐⓗ-RⒺⒺ

I have nothing to declare.

انا معيش حاجة

Ⓐ-Nⓐⓗ MⒾ-ⒺⒺSH HⒶ-Gⓐⓗ

I'm here on business.

انا هنا في شغل

Ⓐ-Nⓐⓗ HⒺ-Nⓐⓗ FⒺⒺ SHⓄGHL

I'm on vacation.

انا في اجازة

Ⓐ-Nⓐⓗ FⒺⒺ ⓐⓗ-GⒶ-Zⓐⓗ

Is there a problem?

في مشكلة؟

FⒺⒺ MⓄⓄSH-KⒺ-Lⓐⓗ

PHRASEMAKER

I'll be staying…

..انا هاقعد

Ⓐ-Nⓐ Hⓐⓘ-ⓞⓦD… (m)
Ⓐ-Nⓐ Hⓐⓘ-ⓞⓦD… (f)

▶ **one night**

ليلة واحدة

LⒶ-Lⓐ WⓐHⓗ-Dⓐ

▶ **two nights**

ليلتين

LⒾL-TⒶN

▶ **one week**

اسبوع واحد

ⒾS-Bⓞⓞⓐ WⓐHⓗ-Hⓔ D

▶ **two weeks**

اسبوعين

ⒾS-Bⓞⓞ-Ⓘ-ⓔN

USEFUL PHRASES

I need a porter.

انا عاوز / انا عاوزة شيال

ⓐ-Nⓐⓗ (ⓘ-WⓘZ SHⓐⓗ-YⓔL (m)

ⓐ-Nⓐⓗ (ⓞⓦ-Zⓐⓗ SHⓐⓗ-YⓔL (f)

These are my bags.

دي شنطي

Dⓔⓔ SHⓄ-Nⓐⓗ-Tⓔⓔ

Can you help me with my luggage?

ممكن تساعدني في الشنط؟

MⓞⓤM-KⓘN Tⓔⓔ-Sⓐⓗ(ⓘD-Nⓔⓔ

Fⓔⓔ ⓔSH-SHⓄ-NⓐⓗT

I'm missing a bag.

في شنطة مش لاقيها / لاقياها

Fⓔⓔ SHⓐⓗN-Tⓐⓗ MⓞⓞSH Lⓔ ⓔ-Hⓐⓗ (m)

Fⓔⓔ SHⓐⓗN-Tⓐⓗ MⓞⓞSH Lⓔ-Yⓔ-Hⓔ (f)

Thank you.   **This is for you.**

شكرا   خد ده ليك

SHⓞⓤK-RⓐⓗN   KHⓞⓤD Dⓐ LⓔⓔK

PHRASEMAKER

Where is...

فين

F@N...

▶ **customs?**

الجمارك؟

@L G@h-M@-R@K

▶ **baggage claim?**

آخد الشنط منين؟

@-KH@D @S-SH@-N@T M@-N@N

▶ **a taxi stand?**

موقف التاكسي؟

M@-'@F @-T@K-S@

▶ **the bus stop?**

محطة الأتوبيس؟

M@-'@F @L @-T@-B@S

HOTEL SURVIVAL

A wide selection of accommodations is available in major cities. The most complete range of facilities is found in five star hotels.

- Make reservations well in advance and request the address of the hotel to be written in Arabic as most taxi drivers do not speak English.

- Try to book a room that is located on a high floor to avoid street traffic noise.

- If you choose to stay out by the pyramids, you may be faced with delays because of constant traffic as well as longer taxi trips.

- Do not leave valuables or cash in your room when you are not there!

- Electrical items like blow-dryers may need an adapter and/or connector. Your hotel may be able to provide one, but to be safe, take one with you.

- It is a good idea to make sure you give your room number to persons you expect to call you. This can avoid confusion with western names.

KEY WORDS

Hotel

فندق

Ⓞ-TⒶL

Bellman

فراش / فراشة

FⒶ-RⒶ́SH

Maid

خدامة

KⒽⒶ-DⒶ́-MⒶ

Message

رسالة

RⒺ-SⒺ́-LⒶ

Reservation

حجز

HⒶGZ

Room service

خدمة الاود

KⒽⒾ́D-MⒾT ⒺL ⓄⒺD

CHECKING IN

My name is…

..انا اسمي

ⓐ-Nⓐh   ①'S-Mⓔⓔ…

I have a reservation.

عندي حجز

(ⓐN-Dⓔⓔ   Hⓐ'GZ

Have you any vacancies?

عندكم حاجة فاضية؟

(ⓐN-Dⓞⓤ-KⓞⓤM
Hⓐ'-Gⓐh   Fⓐh-Dⓔⓔ-ⓐh

What is the charge per night?

بكام في الليلة؟

B①-Kⓐ'M   F①-Lⓔ'-Lⓐh

Is there room service?

في خدمة اود؟

Fⓔⓔ   KⳃⒾ'D-MⒾT   ⓄⓔD

PHRASEMAKER

I would like a room with...

انا عاوز / انا عاوزه اودة...

Ⓐ-Nⓐⓗ (Ⓘ-WⒾ-Z Ⓞ́-Dⓐⓗ... (m)

Ⓐ-Nⓐⓗ (ⓞⓦ-Zⓐⓗ Ⓞ́-Dⓐⓗ... (f)

▸ **one bed**

بسرير واحد

BⓘS-BⓔⓔⓇ WⓐHⓘⓓⒹ

▸ **two beds**

بسريرين

BⓘS-BⓔⓔⓇ-Bⓔ́Ⓝ

▸ **a bathroom**

بحمام

Bⓔⓔ HⓐM-MⓐⓜⓂ

▸ **a shower**

بدش

Bⓔⓔ DⓞⓤSH

▸ **a television**

بتلفزيون

Bⓔⓔ Tⓘ-Lⓘ-VⓘS-Yⓞ́N

USEFUL PHRASES

My room key, please.

مفتاح اودتي لو سمحت؟

M〇〇F-T̃〇ah Ó T-T〇

L〇W S〇-M〇HT

Are there any messages for me?

في اي رسايل ؟

F〇 ① R̃〇-S①-〇L

Where is the dining room?

فين اودة الاكل؟

F〇N Ó-D①T 〇L 〇KL

Are meals included?

بالوجبات؟

B①L-W〇-G〇-B〇T

At what time is breakfast?

الفطار امته؟

〇L-F①-T〇R 〇M-T〇

PHRASEMAKER

(WAKE UP CALL)

Please wake me at...

من فضلك صحيني الساعة

MⓘN FⒶⒹ-LⒶK SⒶH-HⒺⒺ-NⒺ ⒺS-SⒶ)-Ⓐⓗ... (m)

MⓘN FⒶⒹ-LⓘK SⒶH-HⒺⒺ-NⒺ ⒺS-SⒶ)-Ⓐⓗ... (f)

▶ **6:00 a.m.**

ستة الصبح

SⒺT-TⒶ ⒶS-SⓄPH

▶ **6:30 a.m.**

ستة و نص الصبح

SⒺT-TⒶ WⒺ NⓄS ⒶS-SⓄBH

▶ **7:00 a.m.**

سبعة الصبح

SⒶ-BⒶ ⒶS-SⓄBH

▶ **7:30 a.m.**

سبعة و نص الصبح

SⒶ-BⒶ WⒺ NⓄS ⒶS-SⓄBH

▶ **9:00 a.m.**

تسعة الصبح

TⒺ-SⒶ ⒶS-SⓄBH

PHRASEMAKER

I need...

انا محتاج/ انا محتاجة...

ⓐ-Nⓐ MⓐH-TⓔG... (m)

ⓐ-Nⓐ MⓐH-Tⓔ-Gⓐ... (f)

▶ **clean sheets**

ملايات نضيفة

Mⓘ-Lⓘ-YⓔT Nⓘ-DⓔⒺ-Fⓐ

▶ **more blankets**

غطا زيادة

GHⓐ-Tⓐ-TⒺN ZⒺ-Yⓐ-Dⓐ

▶ **more towels**

فوط زيادة

Fⓞ-WⓐT ZⒺ-Yⓐ-Dⓐ

▶ **soap**

صابون

Sⓐ-BⓄⓄN

▶ **ice**

تلج

TⓐLG

▶ **an extra key**

مفتاح زيادة

MꝏF-TⒶH ZEE-YⒶ-Dⓐ

▶ **a hotel safe**

خزنة

KHⒶZ-Nⓐ

▶ **the manager**

المدير

ⒺL Mꝏ-DEER

▶ **a bellman**

الفراش

Fⓐ-Rⓐ'SH

▶ **a maid**

خدامة

KHⓐ-DⒶ-Mⓐ

▶ **a babysitter**

دادة

DⒶ-DⒶ

▶ **toilet paper**

ورق تواليت

Wⓐ-Rⓐ· TWⓐ-LⒾT

PHRASEMAKER

(PROBLEMS)

There is no…

مفيش..

Mⓐ-FⒺSH...

▶ **electricity**

كهربة

KⓐH-Rⓐ-Bⓐ

▶ **heat**

تدفية

TⓐD-FⒶ-Yⓐ

▶ **hot water**

مية سخنة

MⒾ-Yⓐ SⓄKH-Nⓐ

▶ **light**

نور

NⓄⓄR

▶ **toilet paper**

ورق تواليت

Wⓐ-Rⓐ· TWⓐ-LⒾT

PHRASEMAKER

(SPECIAL NEEDS)

Do you have...?

في...

F@...

▶ **an elevator?**

اسانسير؟

@-S@N-S@R

▶ **a ramp?**

مطلعاية؟

M@T-L@-①-Y@

▶ **a wheel chair?**

كرسي بعجل؟

K@R-S@ B①-@-G@L

▶ **facilities for the disabled?**

تسهيلات للمعاقين؟

T①S-H@-L@T
L①L M@-@-K@N

CHECKING OUT

The bill, please.

الفاتورة من فضلك

ⒺL Fⓐh-Tⓞⓞ-Ⓡⓐh MⒾN Fⓐ'D-LⓐK (m)

ⒺL Fⓐh-Tⓞⓞ-Ⓡⓐh MⒾN Fⓐ'D-LⒾK (f)

Is this bill correct?

الفاتورة دي مزبوطة؟

ⒺL Fⓐh-Tⓞⓞ-Ⓡⓐh DⒺⒺ MⓐhZ-Bⓞⓞ-Tⓐh

Do you accept credit cards?

بتقبلو كريديت؟

BⒾ-TⒺⒺ'-Bⓐ'-Lⓞⓞ KRⒺ'-DⒾT KⓐhRT

Could you have my luggage brought down?

ممكن تاخد الشنط تحت من فضلك؟

MⓞⓞM-KⒾN Tⓐ'-HⓞⓞD

Ⓘ-SHⓞ'-NⓐhT TⓐhḦT

MⒾN Fⓐ'D-LⓐK

Please call a taxi.

جيبلي تاكسي من فضلك؟

GƠ-BLEE TƠK-SEE MƠN Fah'D-Lah̊K (m)

GƠ-BEE-LEE TƠK-SEE MƠN Fah'D-LƠK (f)

I had a very good time!

انا قضيت وقت حلو جدا

Ơ-Nah ah̊T-DƠ'T Wah̊T H̊oʊL-oo GƠD-Dah̊N (m)

Ơ-Nah ah̊T-DƠ'T Wah̊T H̊oʊL-oo GƠD-Dah̊N (f)

Thanks for everything.

شكرا علي كل حاجة

SH̊oʊK-Bah̊N (Ơ-Lah̊ KoʊL H̊Ơ-Gah̊

See you next time.

اشوفك المرة الجاية

ah̊-SH̊oo'-Fah̊K ĕL

Mah̊B-Bah̊ ĕL GƠ-Yah̊

Good-bye

مع السلامة

Mah̊ (ƠS-Sah̊-Lĕ'-Mah̊

RESTAURANT SURVIVAL

Most Egyptian cuisine is delicious and is largely influenced by Arabic and Middle-Eastern dishes. It is simple and hearty, made with natural fruits, vegetables, and fresh spices.

- Egyptians eat breakfast between 7 AM and 8 AM and lunch from 1:30 PM to 2:30 PM. Supper is usually served from 7:00 PM to 9:00 PM.

- In many cases some of the least expensive restaurants serve up the tastiest dishes.

- Ahwa "coffee" is a national tradition. It is served in a demitasse cup. Remember to sip slowly so you won't disturb the grounds in the bottom of the cup. If you want your coffee sweetened you must state the amount of sugar you want ahead of time.

- In hotels you may be served Nescafé, an instant coffee that is usually served strong.

- Egyptians also observe the custom of afternoon tea.

- Tipping is accepted.

KEY WORDS

Breakfast

فطار

F@h-T@h'R

Lunch

غدا

GH@'-D@h

Dinner

عشا

(@h'-SH@h

Waiter

جارسون

G@hR-SO'N

Waitress

جارسونة

G@hR-SO'-N@h

Restaurant

مطعم

M@h'T-(@M

USEFUL PHRASES

A table for...

ترابيزة ل

TⓐH-BⓐH-BⒶ-ZⓐH LⒺⒺ

2	4	6
اتنين	اربعة	ستة
'ⒾT-NⒶN	ⓐRB-BⓐH-'ⓐH	Sⓘ-TⓐH

The menu, please.

المنيو من فضلك

ⒺL MⒺN-YⓄⓄ Mⓘン Fⓐ́D-LⓐK (m)

ⒺL MⒺN-YⓄⓄ Mⓘン Fⓐ́D-LⓘK (f)

Separate checks, please.

حساب كل واحد لوحده

H̄Ⓐ-SⓐB KⓄⓊL WⒶ-H̄ⓐD LⓄ-Wⓐ́H̄-DⓄⓄ

Mⓘン Fⓐ́D-LⓐK (m) Mⓘン Fⓐ́D-LⓘK (f)

We are in a hurry.

احنا مستعجلين

ⓐH̄-NⓐH Mⓘ S-Tⓐ-Gⓘ-LⒺⒺN

What do you recommend?

انت تفضل ايه؟

Ⓘ́N-Tⓐ TFⓐD-DⓐL Ⓐ

Please bring us...

ممكن تجيبلنا / تجييبلنا

MⓞⓤM-K①N T①-G①-BLⓐ́-Nⓐⓗ (To a man)

MⓞⓤM-K①N T①-Gⓔⓔ-B①́L-Nⓐⓗ (To a woman)

I'm hungry.

انا جعان / انا جعانة

ⓐ́-Nⓐⓗ G①́-①N (m)

ⓐ́-Nⓐⓗ G①́-ⓐN-ⓐⓗ (f)

I'm thirsty.

انا عطشان / انا عطشانة

ⓐ́-Nⓐⓗ ⓐⓗT-SH@́N (m)

ⓐ́-Nⓐⓗ ⓐⓗT-SH@́-Nⓐⓗ (f)

Is service included?

بالخدمة؟

B①L Kⓗ①́D-Mⓐⓗ

The bill, please.

الفاتورة من فضلك

ⓔL Fⓐ́-Tⓞⓞ́-Rⓐⓗ M①N Fⓐ́D-LⓐⓗK (m)

ⓔL Fⓐ́-Tⓞⓞ́-Rⓐⓗ M①N Fⓐ́D-L①K (f)

EGYPTIAN CUISINES

The remainder of this chapter will help you order foods you are familiar with. On these pages you will find information on Egyptian cuisine.

Cafés offer value but less choice in foods. Stand-up bars offer sandwiches and other on-the-go items.

Local menus are usually published in Arabic and English, except in Alexandria where the menu is published in Arabic and French.

Eating in small Egyptian restaurants presents a great opportunity to use your Say It Right in Arabic phrase book. These small establishments usually serve basic meat and fava-bean fare and waiters speak some English.

Also available are stand-up fast food snack bars. They are quick and inexpensive; however, they may be crowded and you may have to gently push your way up to order.

Make sure to drink bottled water, which is plentiful everywhere, and make sure that the cap is tightly sealed. It is prudent to note that fruit juices may be mixed with local un-filtered water.

EGYPTIAN TRADITION

Most native Egyptians begin their day with a light breakfast including beans, eggs, cheeses, and jams. Lunch is usually between 1:30 PM and 2:30 PM followed by an afternoon tea around 5:00 PM. Suppers are usually late in the evening.

Aysh (bread) is a staple in the Egyptian diet and comes in several varieties. Leavened dough left to rise in the sun is called aysh shams. Plain aysh is a long and skinny loaf. Bread along with rice are featured in most Egyptian main courses.

Egyptian puddings and pastries are usually soaked in sweet syrups. "Fatir" is a stuffed pancake.

Street vendors sell a sandwich made of a smashed "ful" bean filling flavored with a variety of spices. The bean filling is also formed into a patty and fried and placed in bread called ta'miyya in Cairo.

Mezze (something like dip) is served in small dishes with drinks.

BEVERAGE LIST

Coffee

قهوة

ȀH-WȀ

Decaffeinated coffee

قهوة من غير كافايين

ȀH-WȀ MȈN GHȀB KȀ-FȀ-ȆN

Tea

شاي

SHȀ-ȇ

Cream

كريمة

KRȇ-Mah

Sugar

سكر

SȌ-Kah B

Lemon

لمون

Lȁ-MȌN

Milk

لبن

LĂ-BĂN

Hot chocolate

كاكاو سخن

KĂ-Kow SOKHN

Juice

عصير

(ah)-SEE'R

Orange juice

عصير برتقال

(ah)-SEE'R Bour-Too-(ah)'N

Ice water

ميه بتلج

MĬ-Y(ah) BĬT-TĂLG

Mineral water

ميه معدنية

MĬ-Y(ah) M(ah)-DĂ-NEE-Y(ah)

Ice

تلج

TĂLG

AT THE BAR

Bartender

بار مان

B@B-M@N

Cocktail

كوكتيل

K@K-T@L

With ice

بتلج من فضلك

B@ T@LG

Without ice

من غير تلج من فضلك

M@N GH@B T@LG

With lemon

بلمون

B@ L@-M@N

PHRASEMAKER

I would like a glass of...

...ممكن كاس

M⓪M-K①N KⓐS...

▶ **champagne**

شمبانيا

SHⓐM-BⓐN-Yⓐ

▶ **beer**

بيرة

Bⓔⓔ-Rⓐ

▶ **wine**

نبيت

N①-BⓔⓔT

▶ **red wine**

نبيت احمر

N①-BⓔⓔT ⓐH-MⓐR

▶ **white wine**

نبيت ابيض

N①-BⓔⓔT ⓐB-YⓐD

FAMILIAR FOODS

On the following pages you will
find lists of foods you are familiar
with, along with other information
such as basic utensils and preparation
instructions.

A polite way to get a waiter's or waitress's
attention is to say M⓪M-K①N which means **May
I ask?**, followed by your request and thank you.

May I ask...?

ممكن؟

M⓪M-K①N

Please bring me...

ممكن تجيبلي / تجيبيلي

M⓪M-K①N T①-G①-BL⑊... (To a man)

M⓪M-K①N T①-G⑊-B⑊-L⑊... (To a woman)

Thank you

شكرا

SH⓪K-BⓐN

STARTERS

Appetizers

فاتحات شهية

FĀT-ḤĀT SHĒ-HĀ-Yah

Bread and butter

عيش و زبدة

ĀSH WĒ ZĪB-Dah

Cheese

جبنة

GĪB-Nah

Fruit

فاكهة

FĀK-Hah

Salad

سلطة

Sah-Lah-Tah

Soup

شوربة

SHOOB-Bah

MEATS

Bacon

بيكن

BEE-KON

Beef

لحمة

LOH-Mah

Beef steak

ستيك

STAK

Ham

خنزير

KHAN-ZEER

Lamb

ضاني

Dah-NEE

Veal

بتلو

BO-TO-LOO

POULTRY

Baked chicken

فراخ في الفرن

FRŒKH FŒL FŒRN

Grilled chicken

فراخ مشوي

FRŒKH MŒSH-WŒ-ah

Fried chicken

فراخ مقلية

FRŒKH MŒ·-LŒ-Yah

Duck

بط

Bah T

Goose

وز

WŒZ

Turkey

ديك رومي

DŒK RŒŌ-MŒ

SEAFOOD

Fish

سمك

SÃ-MÃK

Lobster

استاكوزا

ÕS-Tah-KÕ-Zah

Oysters

المحار

Mah-HaḧB

Salmon

سلامون

SÃ-LÃ-MÕN

Shrimp

جمبري

GÃM-BÃ-BĒĒ

Trout	**Tuna**
التراوت	سمك تونة
TBOWT	TÕÕ-Nah

OTHER ENTREES

Sandwich

سندويتش

S@ND-W①TCH

Hot dog

هوت دوج

H⊙T D⊙G

Hamburger

هامبرجر

H@M-B⊚B-G℮B

French fries

بطاطس محمرة

B@-T@-T℮S M℮-H@-M@-B@

Pasta

مكرونة

M@-K@-B⊙-N@

Pizza

بتزا

P①D-Z@

VEGETABLES

Carrots

جزر

G@h́-Z@hR

Corn

ذرة

D@ó-R@h

Mushrooms

عش الغراب

(I)SH ① L GH@R-@h́B

Onions	**Garlic**
بصل	توم
B@h́-S@hL	T@uM

Potato

بطاطس

B@h-T@h́-Tẽ́S

Rice	**Tomato**
رزّ	طماطم
R@oZ	Tã́-M@h́-T①M

FRUITS

Apples

تفاح

T@-F@H

Banana

موز

M@-Z@

Grapes

عنب

(@-N@P

Lemon

لمون

L@-M@N

Orange

برتقان

B@R-T@-·@N

Strawberry	**Watermelon**
فراولة	بطيخ
F@-R@-L@	B@-T@KH

DESSERT

Desserts

حلويات

Ḧah-Lah-WEE-ë̈T

Apple pie

فطيرة التّفّاح

Fah-TEE-Ṛit Tou-Fëh

Cherry pie

فطيرة التوت

Fah-TEE-Ṛit Toot

Pastry

عجاين

(I-Gȧ-iN

Candy

كاندي

Kȧn-DEE

Ice cream

ايس كريم

IS KRĒM

Ice cream cone

ايس كريم كونو

IS KRĒM KON

Chocolate

شوكولاته

SHOO-KO-Lah'-Tah

Strawberry

فراولة

Fah-Row'-Lah

Vanilla

فانيليا

Vã-NĒL-Yah

CONDIMENTS

Butter

زبدة

ZÓB-Dah

Ketchup

كاتشاب

KâT-CHÓP

Mayonnaise

مايونيز

Mah-Yoo-NêZ

Mustard

مسطردة

Mous-Tah'B-Dah

Salt	**Pepper**
ملح	فلفل
MahLH	FÓL-FÓL

Sugar

سكر

SÓ-KahB

SETTINGS

Cup

فنجان

FⓘN-GⓐN

Glass

كوباية

Kⓞⓞ-Bⓘ-Yⓔ

Spoon

معلقة

MⓘL-(ⓐ-ⓐh

Fork

شوكة

SHⓞ-Kⓐh

Knife

سكينة

Sⓘ-Kⓔⓔ-Nⓐh

Plate

طبق

Tⓐ-Bⓐh

Napkin

منديل

MⓐN-DⓔⓔL

HOW DO YOU WANT IT COOKED?

Baked

مخبوز

FOL-FORN

Grilled

مشوي

MASH-WEE

Steamed

مستوي علي البخار

BOL BOO-KHAR

Fried

مقلي

MAH-LEE

Medium	**Rare**
نص سوي	سوي قليل
NOOS SO-Wah	SO-Wah A-LEEL

Well done

مستوي

MOS-TO-WEE

PROBLEMS

I didn't order this.

مش ده اللي انا طلبته

MOSH DÃ ĔL Ã-NAH TAH-LAHB-TO

Is the bill correct?

الفاتورة دي مزبوطة؟

ĔL FAH-TOO-RAH DEE MAHZ-BOO-TAH

PRAISE

Thank you for the delicious meal.

شكرا علي الاكل اللذيذ ده

SHOUK-RAN (AH-LAH ÃKL
ĔL LÃ-ZEEZ DÃ

GETTING AROUND

Getting around in a foreign
country can be an adventure
in itself! Taxi and bus drivers
do not always speak English, so
it is essential to be able to give
simple directions. The words
and phrases in this chapter will
help you get where you're going.

- Egypt is considered a safe place to visit and major cities have good transportation.

- It is safer to take a taxi than to drive a car, especially in Cairo.

- Most taxis do not use the meter system, so it is important to negotiate the trip fare before you go.

- Have a map or the address you want to go to written down in Arabic.

- Remember to take a business card from your hotel to give to the taxi driver on your return.

- Train travel is excellent and is connected to major towns and cities. Bus travel is also a convenient way to travel to major towns and cities and is cheaper.

- Alexandria and Cairo have tram or metro systems that run through parts of the city.

KEY WORDS

Airport

مطار

M@n-T@R

Bus Stop

محطة اتوبيس

M@-H@T-T①T @-T@-B€S

Car Rental Agency

مكتب تأجير عربيات

M@K-T@B T@-G€R @-B@-B①-Y@T

Taxi Stand

موقف التاكسي

M@-@F T@K-S€

Train Station

محطة القطر

M@-H@-T①T @L @TB

Subway station

محطة المترو

M@-H@-T①T @L M@-TB@

AIR TRAVEL

A one-way ticket, please.

تذكرة اتجاه واحد

TⓐZ-Kⓐʰ-Rⓐʰ ⓘT-Tⓘ-Gⓐ́ Wⓐ-Ĥⓘ́D
MⓘN FⓐʰD-LⓐʰK (m) MⓘN FⓐʰD-LⓘʰK (f)

A round-trip ticket.

تذكرة رايح جاي

TⓐZ-Kⓐʰ-Rⓐʰ Rⓐʰ-Yⓔ̈Ĥ Gⓘ́-ⒺⒺ

First class

درجة اولى

Dⓐʰ-Rⓐʰ́-Gⓐʰ ⓞⓞ́-Lⓐʰ

How much do I owe?

بكام؟

Bⓘ   Kⓐ́M (m)
Bⓘ   Kⓐ́M (f)

The gate

البوابة

Bⓐʰ-Wⓐ́-Bⓐ̈

PHRASEMAKER

I would like a seat…

انا عاوز / عاوزة كرسي

ȧ-Nah (Ī-WȮZ KOOB-SEE… (m)

ȧ-Nah (OW-Zah KOOB-SEE… (f)

▸ **in first class**

في الدرجة الأولي

FEE ĕ-Dah-Rah-Gah ĕL OO-Lah

▸ **next to the window**

جنب الشباك

GȧNB ȮS-SHȮ-BĕK

▸ **on the aisle**

على الممر

(ah-Lah ĕL Mah-Mah̊R

▸ **near the exit**

جنب الباب

GȧNB ĕL BĕB

BY BUS

Bus

اتوبيس

ⓄⓊ-TⓄⓊ-BⒺⒺ'S

Where is the bus stop?

فين محطة الاتوبيس؟

FⒶN Mⓐ-Ḧⓐ̈T-ⓘT ⒺL ⓄⓊ-TⓄⓊ-BⒺⒺ'S

Do you go to...?

تروح...؟

TⓇⓄⓄḦ...

What is the fare?

كام الاجرة؟

KⓐM ⒺL Ⓞ'-GⓇⓐ

Do I need exact change?

عاوز الفلوس بالظبط؟

(ⓘ-Wⓘz ⒺL FLⓄⓄS BⒺ-Zⓐ'BT (m)

(ⓄⓌW-Zⓐ ⒺL FLⓄⓄS BⒺ-Zⓐ̈BT (f)

PHRASEMAKER

Which bus goes to...

انهي أتوبيس بيروح...

ⓐN-HⒺ ⓞⓤ-Tⓞⓤ-BⒺS Bⓐ-RⓞⓞH...

▶ **the beach?**

الشاطئ؟

ⒺS-SHⓐⓘT

▶ **the market?**

السوق؟

ⒺS-Sⓞⓤˋ

▶ **the airport?**

المطار؟

ⒺL Mⓐ-TⓐⓘR

▶ **Luxor?**

الأقصر؟

Lⓞⓤˋ-SⓞⓤR

▶ **Alexandria?**

إسكندرية؟

ⒺS-KⓐN-DRⓐˊ-Yⓐ

BY CAR

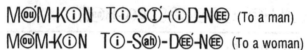

Can you help me?

ممكن تساعدني / تساعديني؟

M(ou)M-K(i)N T(i)-S(i)-(i)D-N(ee) (To a man)

M(ou)M-K(i)N T(i)-S(ah)-D(ee)-N(ee) (To a woman)

My car won't start.

عربيتي مش راضية تدور

(ah)B-B(ee)-(i)-T(ee) M(ou)SH

B(ah)D-D(ee)(ah) T(oo)-D(ou)R

Can you fix it?

تعرف تصلحها؟

T(a)-R(ah)F T(i)-S(ah)L-L(ah)H-H(ah)

What will it cost?

هتتكلف اد ايه؟

H(a)-T(i)T-K(a)-L(i)F (a)D (A)

How long will it take?

هتاخد وقت اد ايه؟

H(a)-T(a)-KH(ou)D W(ah)·T (a)D (A)

PHRASEMAKER

Please check...

ممكن تبص على.

M**ⓐ**M-K**ⓘ**N T**ⓞ**-B**ⓞⓞ**'S...

▶ **the battery**

البطارية

(**ⓐ**)-L**ⓐ** **ⓔ**L B**ⓐ**-T**ⓔ**-R**ⓐ**'-Y**ⓐ**

▶ **the brakes**

الفرامل

ⓔL F**ⓐ**-R**ⓐ**'-M**ⓔ**L

▶ **the oil**

الزيت

(**ⓐ**)-L**ⓐ** **ⓘ**-Z**ⓐ**'T

▶ **the tires**

العجل

(**ⓐ**)-L**ⓐ** **ⓘ**L-(**ⓐ**)-G**ⓔ**L

▶ **the water**

المية

(**ⓐ**)-L**ⓐ** **ⓘ**L-M**ⓘ**'-Y**ⓐ**

SUBWAYS AND TRAINS

Where is the train station?

فين محطة القطر

FAN Mah-Hah-TOT eL ahTB

A one-way ticket, please.

تذكرة اتجاه واحد

TahZ-Kah-Rah O-TO-Gã
Wã-HOD MON FahD-LahK (m)
TahZ-Kah-Rah O-TO-Gã
Wã-HOD MON FahD-LOK (f)

A round-trip ticket.

تذكرة رايح جاى

TahZ-Kah-Rah Rah-YeH GO-EE

First class

درجة اولى

Dah-Rah-Gah oo-Lah

Second class

درجة تانية

Dah-Rah-Gah TahN-Ye

What is the fare?

كام الاجرة؟

KⒶM ⒺL Ⓞ-GⓇⓐh

Is this seat taken?

في حد في الكرسى ده؟

FⒺⒺ HⓐhD FⒾL KⓄⒷ-SⒺⒺ Dⓐh

Do I have to change trains?

لازم اغير القطر؟

LⒶZM ⓐh-GHⓐh-Yⓐh̍Ⓡ ⒺL ⓐhTⓇ

Where are we?

احنا فين؟

ⒶH̍-Nⓐh FⒶN

BY TAXI

Please call a taxi for me.

ممكن تجيبلى / تجيبيلى تاكسي؟

M@M-K①N T①-G①-BL㋎ T㋐K-S㋍ (m)

M@M-K①N T①-G①-B㋍-L㋍ T㋐K-S㋍ (f)

Are you available?

فاضى؟

F㋐-D㋍

I want to go...

..انا عاوز / انا عاوزة اروح

㋐-N㋐ (①-W①Z ((@W-Z㋐) ㋐-R@H...

Stop here, please.

هنا من فضلك

H㋎-N㋐ M①N F㋐D-L㋐K (m)

H㋎-N㋐ M①N F㋐D-L①K (f)

Please wait.

استنى من فضلك

㋎S-T㋐N-N㋐

How much do I owe?

عاوز منى كام؟

(①-W①Z M①N-N㋍ K㋐M

PHRASEMAKER

The simplest way to get to
where you want to go is to
name the destination and say **please**.

▸ **This address...**

...العنوان ده

ⒺL ⒺN-WⒺN Dⓐ...

Have someone at your hotel write down the address
for you in Arabic

▸ **Airport...**

...المطار

ⒺL Mⓐ-Tⓐ́R...

▸ **Subway station...**

...محطة المترو

ⒺL MⒺ-TRⓄ́...

▸ **Luxor...**

...الأقصر

LⓄⓤ-SⓄⓤR...

...please.

...من فضلك

...MⒾN Fⓐ́D-LⓐⒽK (m)
...MⒾN Fⓐ́D-LⒾK (f)

SHOPPING

Whether you plan a major shopping spree or just need to purchase some basic necessities, the following information is useful.

- Upon arriving in Egypt, tourists must fill out a customs declaration form. Keep this with you until you leave as it lists your personal items.

- Cairo International Airport is one of the only airports with a duty-free shop.

- Visitors to Egypt will enjoy shopping for souvenirs or valuable items in the abundant malls. Street markets and small stores are the normal shopping variety in Egypt.

- It is a good idea to purchase some products where they are produced, like the wonderful alabaster made in Luxor.

- Value Added Tax can add 17% to 25% to the original purchase price.

- Shops in Egypt are usually open between the hours of 10:00 AM and 9:00 PM.

KEY WORDS

Credit card

كريديت كارد

KRĒ-DᎥT KᵃᎻRT

Money

فلوس

FLᵒᵒS

Receipt

الوصل

ᎬL WᵃᎻSL

Sale

اوكازيون

Ō-KᵃᎻ-ZᎬᎬ-YᵒᵒN

Store

محل

MᵃᎻ-ḦᵃᎻL

Traveler's checks

شيكات سفر

SHᎬᎬ-KᵃᎿT SᵃᎻ-FᵃᎻR

USEFUL PHRASES

Do you sell…?

بتبيع...

BⓘT-Bⓔ' ...

Do you have…?

عندك؟

ⓐⒽN-DⓐⒽK...

I want to buy...?

انا عاوز اشتري

ⓐ-NⓐⒽ (Ⓘ-WⓘZ ⓐSH-Tⓔ-Rⓔ... (m)

ⓐ-NⓐⒽ (ⓞⓦ-ZⓐⒽ ⓐSH-Tⓔ-Rⓔ... (f)

How much?

بكام؟

Bⓘ-KⓐM

I´m just looking.

انا بس بتفرج

ⓐ-NⓐⒽ BⓐS BⓔT-FⓐⒽR-RⓐⒽG

When do the shops open?

المحلات بتفتح امته؟

ⓔL MⓐⒽ-ⒽⓐⒽ-LⓔT
Bⓘ-TⓘF-TⓐⒽⒽ ⓔM-TⓐⒽ

No, thank you.

لا شكرا

LĀ· SH@K-B@N

Can't you give me a discount?

مش ممكن تديني خصم؟

M①SH M@M-K①N
T@-D@-N@ KH@SM

I'll take it.

هاخدها

HĀ K@D HĀ

I would like a receipt please.

انا عاوز فاتورة من فضلك

@-N@ ①-W①Z F@-T@-B@
M①N F@D-L@K (man to man)

@-N@ ①-W①Z F@-T@-B@
M①N F@D-L①K (man to woman)

@-N@ @-Z@ F@-T@-B@
M①N F@D-L①K (woman to woman)

@-N@ @-Z@ F@-T@-B@
M①N F@D-L@K (woman to man)

SHOPS AND SERVICES

Bakery

فرن

F⊙RN

Bank

بنك

B@NK

Hair salon / Barbershop

حلاق

H̃@L

Jewelry store

جواهرجي

G@h-W@h-HⒺ'R-GⒺ

Bookstore

مكتبة

M@K-T@h́-B@h

News stand

بياع الجرايد

B@h-Y⊙')-GH@h-Y⊚D

Camera shop

مصوراتي

M@h-S⊙-W@h-R@h-TⒺ

Pharmacy

صيدلية

S①-D@h-L@'-Y@h

SHOPPING LIST

On the following pages you will find some common items you may need to purchase on your trip.

Aspirin

أسبرين

@S-P@-R@N

Cigarettes

سجاير

S@-G@-Y@R

Deodorant

مزيل عرق

M@-Z@L (@-R@·

Dress

فستان

F@S-T@N

Film (camera)

فلم

F@LM

Memory stick (digital camera)

فلاش ميموري

FL@SH M@-M@-R@

Perfume

برفان

P@R-F@N

Razor blade

مكنة حلاقة

M@-K@-N@T H@-L@'

Shampoo

شامبو

SH@M-B@

Shaving cream

كريم حلاقة

KR@M H@-L@'

Shirt

قميص

'@-M@S

Sunglasses

نضارة شمس

N@-D@-R@T SH@MS

Suntan oil

زيت صن تان

ZAT SAHN-TAN

Toothbrush

فرشاة الأسنان

FOR-SHOT SE-NEN

Toothpaste

معجون الأسنان

MAH-GOON SE-NEN

Water

مية

MI-Yah

Water (mineral)

مية معدنية

MI-Yah MAH-DE-NA-Yah

ESSENTIAL
SERVICES

THE BANK

As a traveler in a foreign country your primary contact with banks will be to exchange money.

- The unit of currency in Egypt is the **Egyptian Pound (LE/£E).** The best place to change currency is banks; however, there are Forex bureaux "foreign exchange bureaus" that can be found in most cities that will also change currency.

- One Egyptian pound equals 100 piastres. Note denominations are LE1 (brown), LE5 (blue), LE10 (red), LE20 (green), LE50 (red), and LE100 (green). Coin values are 5pt, 10pt, 20pt, 25pt, and 50pt

- Take time to familiarize yourself with different bank notes and their respective values.

- It is a good idea to carry traveler's checks rather than cash. Don't display money in public.

- Have your passport handy when changing money.

KEY WORDS

Bank

بنك

B@NK

Exchange office

مكتب صرافة

M@K-T@B @S-S@-B@'-F@

Money

فلوس

FL@S

Traveler's check

شيك سفر

SH@K S@'-F@B

USEFUL PHRASES

Where is the bank?

فين البنك

FⒶN ⒺL BⒶNK

At what time does the bank open?

البنك بيفتح امته؟

ⒺL BⒶNK BⒺⒺ-YⒺF-TⒶH ⒺM-TⒶ

Where is the exchange office?

فين مكتب الصرافة؟

FⒶN MⒶK-TⒶB Ⓔ-SⒾ-ⓇⒶF-Ⓕah

What time does the exchange office open?

مكتب الصرافة بيفتح امتة؟

MⒶK-TⒶB ⒺS-SⒾ-ⓇⒶF-Ⓕah
BⒺⒺ-YⒺF-TⒶH ⒺM-TⒶ

Can I change dollars here?

ممكن اغير دولارات هنا؟

MⓄⓊM-KⒾN Ⓐh-GHⒾ-ⒶⓇ
DⓄ-LⒶh-ⓇⒶT HⒺ-Nah

What is the exchange rate?

كام سعر الصرف؟

KⒶM SⒺ)R ⒺS-SⓐRF

I would like large bills.

انا عاوز / انا عاوزة عملة كبيرة

Ⓐ-Nⓐⓗ (Ⓘ-WⓘZ ⓄM-Lⓐⓗ KⓘBⒺⒺ-Rⓐⓗ (m)

Ⓐ-Nⓐⓗ (ⓞⓦ-Zⓐⓗ ⓄM-Lⓐⓗ KⓘBⒺⒺ-Rⓐⓗ (f)

I would like small bills.

انا عاوز / انا عاوزة عملة صغيرة

Ⓐ-Nⓐⓗ (Ⓘ-WⓘZ ⓄM-Lⓐⓗ

SⓄ-GHⓘ-Yⓐⓗ-Rⓐⓗ (m)

Ⓐ-Nⓐⓗ (ⓞⓦ-Zⓐⓗ ⓄM-Lⓐⓗ

SⓄ-GHⓘ-Yⓐⓗ-Rⓐⓗ (f)

I need change.

انا عاوز / انا عاوزة فكة

Ⓐ-Nⓐⓗ (Ⓘ-WⓘZ FⒶK-Kⓐⓗ (m)

Ⓐ-Nⓐⓗ (ⓞⓦ-Zⓐⓗ FⒶK-Kⓐⓗ (f)

Do you have an ATM?

عندكم ايه تي ام

(ⒶN-Dⓞⓞ-KⓞⓞM   Ⓐ-TⒺⒺ-ⒺM

POST OFFICE

If you are planning on sending
letters and postcards, be sure
to send them early so that you
don't arrive home before they do.

KEY WORDS

Air mail

بريد جوي

BĀ-RĒD GĀ-WĒ

Letter

جواب

GĀ-WĀB

Post office

بوسطة

BŌS-Tah

Postcard

كارت معايدة

KahRT MO-Ī-Dah

Stamp

طابع

TĀ-Bi)

USEFUL PHRASES

Where is the post office?

فين البوسطة؟

FᎪN ⒺL BⓄS-Tⓐh

What time does the post office open?

البوسطة بتفتح امته؟

ⒺL PⓄS-Tⓐh Bⓘ-TⓘF-TⓐhⱧ ⒺM-Tⓐh

I need stamps.

انا عاوز / انا عاوزة طوابع

ⓐN-ⓐh (Ⓘ-WⓘZ Tⓐh-Wⓐ-Bⓐ) (m)

ⓐN-ⓐh (ⓄⱲ-Zⓐh Tⓐh-Wⓐ-Bⓐ) (f)

I need envelopes.

انا عاوز / انا عاوزة ظرف

ⓐ-Nⓐh (Ⓘ-WⓘZ ZⓐhⱤF (m)

ⓐ-Nⓐh (ⓄⱲ-Zⓐh ZⓐhⱤF (f)

I need a pen.

انا عاوز / انا عاوزة قلم

ⓐ-Nⓐh (Ⓘ-WⓘZ ⓐ-LⓐhM (m)

ⓐ-Nⓐh (ⓄⱲ-Zⓐh ⓐ-LⓐhM (f)

TELEPHONE

Placing phone calls in Egypt can be
a test of will and stamina! Besides
the obvious language barriers, service
can vary greatly from one city to the
next.

- You should be able to use your cell
  phone in Egypt if your company has an
  agreement with local operators, but the
  roaming charges can be high.

- You can purchase a local SIM card
  and pay-as-you-go set for a reasonable
  price and it will include an Egypt phone
  number.

- In Egypt you can purchase calling cards
  to use in local call boxes.

- Internet cafes are usually well located
  and available in major cities and in many
  hotels.

KEY WORDS

Telephone

تليفون

T(ĕ)-L(EE)-F(O)N

Information

الدليل

(i)D-D(ä)-L(EE)L

Long distance (call)

دولي

D(ah)-WL(EE)

Operator

مشغل

M(oo)-SH(ah)-GH(i)L

Phone book

دليل التليفون

D(ä)-L(EE)L (i)-T(ĕ)-L(EE)-F(O)N

Public telephone

تليفون عمومي

T(ĕ)-L(EE)-F(O)N (O)-M(oo)-M(EE)

USEFUL PHRASES

Where is the telephone?

فين التليفون؟

FⒶN Ⓘ-TⒺ-LⒺⒺ-FⓄN

Where is the public telephone?

فين تليفون عمومي هنا؟

FⒶN TⒺ-LⒺⒺ-FⓄN
Ⓞ-MⓄⓄ-MⒺⒺ HⒺ-Nⓐⓗ

May I use your telephone?

ممكن استخدم تليفونك؟

MⓄⓄM-KⓄN ⓐS-TⓐKⓗ-DⓘM
TⒺ-LⒺⒺ-FⓄ-NⒺK

Operator, I don't speak Arabic.

انا مبتكلمش عربي

ⓐ-Nⓐⓗ MⓘSH BⓐT-KⓐL-LⒺM
ⓐⓗ-Ⓡⓐⓗ-BⒺⒺ

I want to call this number...

...انا عاوز / عاوزة اتصل بالنمرة دي

ⓐ-Nⓐ (Ⓘ́-WⓘZ (m)

ⓐ-Nⓐ (ⓞⓦ́-Zⓐ (f)

ⓐ-Tⓐ-Sⓐ́L Bⓘ-Nⓘ́M-Bⓐ Dⓔⓔ...

SIGHTSEEING AND ENTERTAINMENT

The official name of Egypt is Arab Republic of Egypt and Cairo is the capital. Apart from showcasing one of the seven wonders of the world, Cairo offers museums, art, cinema, live theater, and night clubs.

THE GREAT PYRAMIDS OF GIZA

The illustration below depicts one of the pyramids located in the great pyramid complex of Giza. The pyramid of Khafre and the great sphinx of Giza are located approximately twelve and a half miles from Giza.

Khafre's pyramid is the second largest pyramid in Giza and is also the tomb of fourth-dynasty Pharaoh Khafre.

KEY WORDS

Admission

دخول

DO-KHOOL

Map

خريطة

KHah-REE-Tah

Reservation

حجز

HahGZ

Ticket

تذكرة

Tah-Kah-Rah

Tour

جولة

GoW-Lah

Tour guide

مرشد

MooB-SHiD

USEFUL PHRASES

Where is the tourist agency?

فين مكتب السياحة؟

FⒶN MⒶK-TⓐB
ⒺS-SⒺE-Yⓐ-Ⓗⓐ

Where do I buy a ticket?

منين اشتري تذكرة؟

MⒾ-NⒶN ⓐSH-TⒺ-ⒷEE TⓐZ-Kⓐ-Ⓡⓐ

How much?

بكام؟

BⒾ-KⒶ́M

How long?

اد ايه؟

ⓐD Ⓐ

When?

امتى؟

Ⓔ́M-Tⓐ

Where?

فين؟

FⒶN

Do I need reservations?

انا محتاج احجز؟

ⓐ-Nⓐⓗ Mⓐ̈H-Tⓔ̈G ⓐⓗH-GⓘZ

Does the guide speak English?

هل المرشد بيتكلم انجليني؟

ⓔL MⓞⓞB-SHⓔ̈D BⓘT-Kⓐ̈-LⓘM
ⓔⓔN-GLⓔⓔ-Zⓔⓔ

How much do children pay?

الاطفال يدفعو كام؟

ⓔL ⓐT-FⓐⓗL Yⓔ̈D-Fⓐ̈-ⓞⓞ Kⓐ̈M

I need your help.

انا عاوز / عاوزة مساعدة

ⓐ́-Nⓐⓗ (ⓘ-Wⓘ̀Z Mⓞⓞ-Sⓐⓗ)-Dⓘ-Tⓐ̈K (m)
ⓐ́-Nⓐⓗ (ⓞⓦ̀-Zⓐⓗ Mⓞⓞ-Sⓐⓗ)-Dⓘ-Tⓐ̈K (f)

Thank you.

شكرا

SHⓞⓤ́K-BⓐⓗN

PHRASEMAKER

May I invite you to…

ممكن اعزمك / اعزمك على

MⓄⓊM-KⒾN ⓐ-ZⒾ'M-ⓐK (ⓐ'-Lⓐ...(m)
MⓄⓊM-KⒾN ⓐ-ZⓄ'M-ⓘK (ⓐ'-Lⓐ...(f)

▶ **a concert?**

حفلة؟

Hⓐ'-FLⓐ

▶ **dinner?**

عشا؟

(ⓐ'-SHⓐ

▶ **the movies?**

السينما؟

ⒾS-SⒾ'-NⒺ-Mⓐ

▶ **the theatre?**

المسرح؟

ⒾL-Mⓐ'S-Rⓐ'Ĥ

Note: The above phrases are appropriate in a situation where you are in a circle of friends. They are not for use on a first meeting or for new acquaintances.

PHRASEMAKER

I'm looking for...

انا بدور على...

ⓐ-Nⓐⓗ Bⓐ-Dⓞⓦ-WⓐⓗⓇ (ⓐⓗ)-Lⓐⓗ...

▶ **the health club**

الجيم؟

JⓘM

▶ **the swimming pool**

حمام السباحة؟

Hⓐⓗ-Mⓞⓜ Sⓔ-Bⓐⓗ-Hⓐⓗ

▶ **the tennis court**

ملعب تنس؟

Mⓐ-LⓐⓗB Tⓔ-NⓔS

▶ **the golf course**

ملعب جولف؟

Mⓐ-LⓐⓗB GⓞLF

HEALTH

Hopefully you will not need
medical attention on your
trip. If you do, it is important
to communicate basic information
regarding your condition.

- Check with your insurance
  company before leaving home
  to find out if you are covered in a
  foreign country. You may want to purchase
  traveler's insurance before leaving home.

- If you take prescription medicine, carry
  your prescription with you. Have your
  prescriptions translated into Arabic writing
  before you leave home.

- Take a small first-aid kit with you. You may
  want to include basic cold and anti-diarrhea
  medications. However, you should be able
  to find most items like aspirin locally.

- Carry tissue with you as it is not always
  provided in Egyptian washrooms. Sometimes
  there will be an attendant offering a napkin
  to dry your hands. Tipping is accepted in
  this situation.

- Hospitals are more accessible in cities. You
  can also contact your local embassy for
  information about finding a doctor.

KEY WORDS

Ambulance

إسعاف

ⓘL-·ⓘS-ⓐF

Dentist

دكتوراسنان

DⓞK-TⓞB ·ⓐS-NⓐN

Doctor

دكتور

DⓞK-TⓞB

Hospital

مستشفى

Mⓞⓞ S-Tⓐ SH-Fⓐ h

Prescription

روشتة

Bⓞⓞ-SHⓔ T-Tⓐ h

USEFUL PHRASES

I am sick.

انا تعبان / انا تعبانة

ⓐ-Nⓐ (ⓐ-YⒺN (m)

ⓐ-Nⓐ (ⓐ-YⒺN-ⓐ (f)

I'm pregnant.

انا حامل

ⓐ-Nⓐ Ḧⓐ-MⓘL

I'm diabetic.

انا عندى سكر

ⓐ-Nⓐ Mⓐ-RⒺD
Bⓘs-Sⓞ-Kⓐⓡ (m)

ⓐ-Nⓐ Mⓐ-RⒺ-Dⓐ
Bⓘs-Sⓞ-Kⓐⓡ (f)

In Egypt the phrase "I am hurt" is not used. You would just state the area of pain, such as head, stomach, arm, leg, etc.

I'm allergic to...

انا عندى حساسية ضد

@h́-N@h (@h́N-D⒠

Ḧⓐ-Sⓐ́S-Yⓐ M⒤N...

I have a heart condition.

انا عندى مشاكل في القلب

ⓐ́-N@h F⒤L-⒠LB Mⓐ́-SHⓐ-K⒤L (m)

ⓐ́-N@h (@h́N-D⒠ Mⓐ́-SHⓐ-K⒤L (f)

It's an emergency!

دى حالة طوارئ

D⒠ T@h-W@h́-B⒤

Call an ambulance!

اطلب / اطلبى الإسعاف

ⓔ́T-LⓄB ⓔL ⓔ́S-S⒤-(ⓔF (To a man)

ⓔ́T-LⓄ́-B⒠ ⓔL ⓔ́S-S⒤-(ⓔF (To a woman)

PHRASEMAKER

I need...

‫...انا عاوز / انا عاوزة‬

ⓐ-Nⓐₕ (Ⓘ-WⓘZ... (m)

ⓐ-Nⓐₕ (ⓞⓦ-Zⓐₕ... (f)

▶ **a doctor**

‫دكتور / دكتورة‬

DⓞⓤK-TⓞⓇ (m)

DⓞⓤK-TⓞⓇ (f)

▶ **a dentist**

‫دكتور اسنان‬

DⓞⓤK-TⓞⓇ ·ⓐS-NⓐN

▶ **an optician**

‫دكتور عيون‬

DⓞⓤK-TⓞⓇ (Ⓞ-YⓞⓞN

---

a nurse

‫ممرضة‬

Mⓞⓞ-Mⓐₕ-Ⓡⓔ̌-Dⓐₕ

---

a pharmacy

‫صيدلية‬

SⒾ-Dⓐₕ-LⒾ-Yⓐₕ

PHRASEMAKER
(AT THE PHARMACY)

Do you sell...

عندك...

(ⓐN-DⓐK...

▸ **aspirin?**

أسبرين؟

ⓐS-PⒺⒺ-RⒺⒺN

▸ **Band-Aids?**

بلاستر؟

BLⓐS-TⓐR

▸ **cough syrup?**

دوا كحة؟

Dⓐ-Wⓐ KⓄ-Hⓐ

▸ **ear drops?**

نقط للودان؟

NⓄ-•ⓐT LⒾL WⒾ-DⓐN

▸ **eye drops?**

نقط للعيون؟

NⓄ-•ⓐT LⒾL (ⓐN

BUSINESS TRAVEL

It is important to show appreciation and interest in another person's language and culture, particularly when doing business. A few well-pronounced phrases can make a great impression.

- Exchanging business cards is very important, so be sure to bring a good supply with you.

- It is a good idea to have your business card printed in Arabic.

- Present your business card with the Arabic side up.

- When you receive a card, be sure to examine it and then place it in your card case.

- It is customary to give and receive hand shakes when greeting, but it is a good idea to follow the lead of your Egyptian business counterpart.

- When trying to get someone's attention call them by name, as summoning with a hand is considered rude.

- In most cases you should address your Egyptian business counterparts by their title followed by surname.

- Business dress is conservative for both men and women.

KEY WORDS

Appointment (business)

موعد

MⒾ-ⓐD

Business card

الكارت

KⓐRT

Meeting

إجتماع

ⒾG-TⒾ-MⒶ

Marketing department

قسم تسويق

KⒾS-ⓤⓝM Ⓘ-TⓐS-WⒺⒺ·

Office   **Presentation**

مكتب   تقديم

MⓐK-TⓐB   Tⓐ-DⒺⒺM

Telephone

تليفون

TⒺ-LⒺⒺ-FⓄN

USEFUL PHRASES

I have an appointment.

انا عندي موعد

ⓐ-Nⓐⓗ　(ⓐⓗ-DⒺⒺ　Mⓘ-ⓐD

My name is…

انا اسمي..

ⓐ-Nⓐⓗ　ⓘ́S-MⒺⒺ…

Pleased to meet you.

فرصة سعيدة

'ⓘT-SH́ⓐ̀B-B̀ⓐ̀F-Nⓐⓗ

Here is my card.

ده الكارت بتاعى

Dⓐⓗ　ⓔ̈L　Kⓐ̀BT　Bⓘ-Tⓐ-'ⒺⒺ

Can we get an interpreter?

ممكن مترجم؟

Mⓐ́M-Kⓘ̀N　Mⓐⓤ-Tⓐ̈B-Gⓘ̀M

Can you write your address for me?

ممكن تكتب عنوانك؟

MOUM-KON TĒK-TŌB-LEE
(ON-WĒ-NĒK (To a man)

MOUM-KON TĒK-TĒ-BEE-LEE
(ON-WĒ-NĪK (To a woman)

Can you write your phone number?

ممكن تكتب رقم تليفونك؟

MOUM-KON TĒK-TŌB-LEE RAH-KAHM
TĒ-LĒ-FŌ-NĒK (To a man)

MOUM-KON TĒK-TŌB-LEE RAH-KAHM
TĒ-LĒ-FŌ-NĪK (To a woman)

This is my phone number.

ده رقم تليفونى

DUH RAH-KAHM TĒ-LĒ-FŌ-NEE

Good-bye.

مع السلامة

MAH (ĀS-SAH-LĒ-MAH

PHRASEMAKER

I need...

انا عاوز / انا عاوزة...

@-N@h (①-W①Z...

@-N@h (ⓞⓦ-Z@h...

▶ **a computer**

كمبيوتر

K①M-B㊄ⓞⓞ-T①R

▶ **a copy machine**

مكنة تصوير

M@-K@h-N①T T@hS-W㊄R

▶ **a fax or fax machine**

مكنة فاكس

M@-K@h-N①T F@KS

▶ **a lawyer**

محامى

M①-H①-M㊄

▶ **an interpreter**

مترجم

M①-T@R-G①M

▶ **a notary**

كاتب

KǍ-TⒾB

▶ **a conference room**

اودة اجتماعات

Ⓞ-DⒾT ⒾG-TⒺ-MⒾ-ⒺT

▶ **stamps**

طوابع

Tⓐⓗ-Wⓐⓗ-BⓐⒶ)

▶ **typing paper**

ورق كتابة

WⒶ-Rⓐⓗ· KⒺⒺ-TⒶ-Bⓐⓗ

GENERAL INFORMATION

Egypt has two seasons, winter and summer. Winters are very cold. May, June, September, and October offer the best weather because they are usually dry and mild.

SEASONS

Spring

الربيع

(iB-Rah-BEE)

Summer

الصيف

(i)-SAF

Autumn

الخريف

(i)L-KHa-REEF

Winter

الشتا

(i)S-SHi-Tah

THE DAYS

Monday

الإتنين

①-L①T-N②N

Tuesday

التلات

①-T③-L⑥T

Wednesday

الأربع

①L-·④R-B④)

Thursday

الخميس

①L-K④-M⑥S

Friday

الجمعة

①L-G①-M④

Saturday

السّبت

⑥S-S④BT

Sunday

الحد

①L-H③D

THE MONTHS

January

يناير

YⒶ-NⒺ-YⒾR

February

فبراير

FⒾB-RⒺ-YⒾR

March

مارس

MⒺ-RⒾS

April

إبريل

ⒶB-RⒺEL

May

مايو

MⒶ-Y⒪⒪

June

يونيه

Y⒪⒪N-Y⒪⒪

July

يوليه

Y⒪⒪L-Y⒪⒪

August

أغسطس

Ⓞ-GH⒪⒪S-T⒪⒪S

September

سبتمبر

SⒾB-TⒶM-BⒾR

October

أكتوبر

⒪⒪K-T⒪⒪-BahR

November

نوفمبر

N⒪⒪-VⒾM-BⒾR

December

ديسمبر

DⒾ-SⒾM-BⒾR

COLORS

Black	**White**
أسود	أبيض
ⓘS-WⓘD	ⓐⒽB-Yⓐ́D
Blue	**Brown**
ازرق	بني
ⓐ́Z-Rⓐ'	Bⓞ́ⓞN-NⒺⒺ
Gray	**Gold**
رمادي	دهبي
Rⓐ-Mⓐ́Ⓗ-DⒺⒺ	Dⓐ́-Hⓐⓐ́-BⒺⒺ
Orange	**Yellow**
برتقاني	أصفر
Bⓞ́ⓞR-Tⓞⓞ-·ⓐⒽ-NⒺⒺ	ⓐ́S-Fⓐ́ⒽR
Red	**Green**
أحمر	أخضر
ⓐ́Ⓗ-Mⓐ́ⒽR	ⓐ́ⓀⒽ-Dⓐ́ⒽR
Pink	**Purple**
وردي	أرجواني
Wⓐ́ⒽR-DⒺⒺ	ⓔR-Gⓞ́ⓞ-Wⓐ́-NⒺⒺ

Colors on this page are shown in masculine form. Both masculine (m) and feminine (f) forms are shown in the dictionary.

NUMBERS

0	**1**	**2**	**3**
زيرو	واحد	اتنين	تلات
ZEE-RO	WE-HID	IT-NAN	TA-LE-Tah

4	**5**	**6**	**7**
اربعة	خمسة	ستة	سبعة
ahR-Bah-ah	KHaM-Sa	Si-Tah	SaB-ah

8	**9**	**10**
تمانيه	تسعة	عشرة
Tah-Ma-NYah	TiS-ah	ah-SHah-Bah

11	**12**
حداشر	اتناشر
He-Dah-SHahR	iT-Nah-SHahR

13	**14**
تلاتاشر	اربعتاشر
Ta-Lah-Tah-SHahR	ahR-Bah-Tah-SHahR

15	**16**
خمستاشر	ستاشر
KHah-MahS-Tah-SHahR	Si-Tah-SHahR

17	**18**
سبعتاشر	تمنتاشر
Sa-Bah-Tah-SHahR	Ta-MaN-Tah-SHahR

19	20
تسعتاشر	عشرين
TⓘS-Sⓐh)-Tⓐh-SHⓐhR	(ⓐSH-RⒺⓝN

30	40
تلاتين	اربعين
Tⓐ-Lⓐ-TⒺⓝN	ⓐR-Bⓘ-(ⒺⓝN

50	60
خمسين	ستين
KHⓐM-SⒺⓝN	SⓘT-ⒺⓝN

70	80
سبعين	تمانين
Sⓐ-Bⓐh-(ⒺⓝN	Tⓐ-Mⓐh-NⒺⓝN

90	100
تسعين	مية
TⓘS-(ⒺⓝN	MⒺⓝ-Yⓐ

1,000	1,000,000
الف	مليون
'ⓐLF	MⒺⓝL-YⓞⓝN

DICTIONARY

Each English entry is followed by the Arabic script followed by the EPLS Vowel Symbol System. Masculine words will be followed by (m) and feminine will be followed by an (f) respectively.

A

a lot كتير K①-T❡R

able (to be) قادر ❡-D①R / ⓐD-Rⓐ

accident حادثة H❡D-S❡

accommodation سكن Sⓐ-KⓐN

account حساب H①-SⓐB

address عنوان ①N-WⓐN

admission دخول D⓪-K⒣⓪L

afraid (to be) خايف / خايفة K⒣❡-Y①F / K⒣①-Fⓐ

after بعد Bⓐ)D

afternoon بعد الظّهر Bⓐ)D ①D-D⓪HB

air-conditioning تكييف TⓐK-Y❡F

aircraft طيارة T①-Yⓐ-Rⓐ

airline طيران Tⓐ-Yⓐ-RⓐN

airport مطار Mⓐ-TⓐB

aisle ممرّ M@h-M@hB

Algeria الجزاير ①G-G@-Z@-Y①B

Algerian (m) جزايري G@-Z@-B⒠⒠

Algerian (f) جزايرية G@-Z@-B⒠⒠-Y@h

all كلّ K⒪L

almost تقريبًا T@h-B⒠⒠-B@N

alone لوحدي L①-W@-D⒠⒠

also كمان K@h-M@N

always دايما D①-M@N

ambulance إسعاف ·①S-(@)F

America امريكا @M-B⒠⒠-K@h

American (m) أمريكى @M-B⒠⒠-K⒠⒠

American (f) أمريكية @M-B⒠⒠-K①@h

Americans امريكان @M-B⒠⒠-K@N

and و W①

another تانى / تانية T@-N⒠⒠ / T@-N①@h

anything اى حاجة ① H@-G@

apartment شقّة SH@h·-·@h

appetizers فاتحات شّهيّة M@-Z@h

apple تفّاحة T⒪F-F@–Ħ@h

appointment معاد M①-(@)D

April إبريل @B-B⒠⒠L

arrival وصول   W◎-S◎L

ashtray طفاية سجاير   T◎F-F◎-Y◎T S◎-G◎-Y◎R

aspirin أسبرين   ◎S-B◎-R◎N

attention انتباه   ◎N-T◎-B◎H

August أغسطس   ◎-GH◎S-T◎S

Australia استراليا   ◎-STR◎-LY◎

Australian (m) استرالي   ◎S-T◎-R◎-LEE

Australian (f) استرالية   ◎S-T◎-R◎-L◎◎

author (m) مؤلَّف   M◎-·◎L-L◎F

author (f) مؤلَّفة   M◎-·◎L-L◎F-◎

autumn خريف   KH◎-R◎F

avenue طريق   T◎-R◎·

awful (m) فظيع   F◎-Z◎)

awful (f) فظيعة   F◎-Z◎-(◎)

B

baby (m) طفل   T◎FL

baby (f) طفلة   T◎-FL◎

babysitter دادة   D◎-D◎

bacon بيكن   B◎-K◎N

bad (m) وحش   W◎-H◎SH

bad (f) وحشة   W◎H-SH◎

bag شنطة   SH◎N-T◎

baggage شنط SHⓌ-NⓐT

Bahrain البحرين ⒺL-BⓐⒽ-RⒺN

Bahraini (m) بحرينى BⓐⒽ-RⒶ-NⒺ

Bahraini (f) بحرينية BⓐⒽ-RⒶ-NⒾⓐ

baked مخبوز / مخبوزة FⒾL-FⓄBN

bakery فرن FⓄBN

banana موز MⓄZ

Band-Aid بلاستر BLⓐS-TⓐB

bank بنك BⓐNK

barber حلاق ⒽⓐL-LⒶ·

bartender بار مان BⓐB-MⓐN

bath حمّام ⒽⓐM-MⓐM

bathtub بانيو BⓐN-YⓄ

bathroom تواليت TWⓐ-LⒾT

battery بطّاريّة BⒶ-TⒶ-BⒺ-Yⓐ

beach شاطئ SHⓐT

beautiful (m) جميل GⒶ-MⒺL

beautiful (f) جميلة GⒶ-MⒺ-Lⓐ

because عشان (Ⓐ-SHⓐN

bed سرير SⒶ-RⒺB

beer بيرة BⒺ-Bⓐ

bellman منادي MⓄ-NⒶ-DⒺ

belt حزام ⒽⒾ-ZⓐM

big (m)   كبير   KⒾ-BⒺⒺB

big (f)   كبيرة   KⒾ-BⒺⒺ-Bⓐh

bill   فاتورة   Fⓐh-TⓄⓄ-Rⓐh

black (m)   أسود   ⒶS-WⒾD

black (f)   سودة   SⓄ-Dⓐh

blanket   بطّانيّة   Bⓐ-Tⓐ-NⒺⒺ-Yⓐh

blue (m)   أزرق   ⓐZ-Rⓐh•

blue (f)   زرقة   Zⓐh-•ⓐh

boat   قارب   ⓐ-RⒾB

book   كتاب   KⒾ-Tⓐ B

bookstore   مكتبة   MⓐK-Tⓐ-Bⓐh

border   حدود   Ḧⓔ-DⓄⓄD

boy   ولد   Wⓐ-Lⓐ D

bracelet   إسورة   ⒾS-Wⓔ-Rⓐh

bread   عيش   ⒶSH

breakfast   فطار   Fⓐ-Tⓐ B

broiled (m)   مشوى   MⓐSH-WⒺⒺ

broiled (f)   مشوية   MⓐSH-WⒾ-Yⓐh

brother   أخ   ⓐK̲H̲

brown (m)   بنى   BⓄⓄN-NⒺⒺ

brown (f)   بنية   BⓄⓄN-NⒾⓐh

brush   فرشة   FⓄB-SHⓐh

building   مبنى   Mⓐ B-Nⓐh

bus اتوبيس ’ⓞⓤ-Tⓞⓤ-BⒺⒺS

bus station موقف الأتوبيس Mⓐⓦ-ⓐF ’ⓞⓤ-Tⓞⓤ-BⒺⒺS

bus stop محطة الأتوبيس Mⓐ-Ⓗⓐ̈T-TⓘT ’ⓞⓤ-Tⓞⓤ-BⒺⒺS

business شغل SHⓞGHL

butter زبدة Zⓘ̈B-Dⓐ

buy (to) يشتري Yⓘ̈SH-Tⓘ̈-RⒺⒺ

C

cab تاكسي Tⓐ̈K-SⒺⒺ

café قهوة ’ⓐ̈H-Wⓐ

camel جمل Gⓐ-Mⓐ̈L

camera كاميرا Kⓐ̈-Mⓐ-Bⓐⓗ

Canada كندا Kⓐ̈-Nⓐ-Dⓐⓗ

Canadian (m) كندي Kⓐ-Nⓐ-DⒺⒺ

Canadian (f) كندية Kⓐ-Nⓐ-Dⓘ̈ⓐⓗ

car عربية (ⓐⓗ-Rⓐ-BⒺⒺ-Yⓐ)

carrot جزر Gⓐⓗ-ZⓐⓗB

castle قلعة ’ⓐ̈-Lⓐⓗ

cathedral كاثرائية Kⓐ̈-TⓘT-DBⓐⓗ-Ⓐ-Yⓐⓗ

celebration إحتفال ⓐⒽ-Tⓐ-Fⓐ̈L

center وسط Wⓘ̈ST

cereal (cold) سيريل Sⓘ̈-Bⓘ̈L

chair كرسي KⓞⓞB-SⒺⒺ

champagne شمبانيا SHⓐⓗM-BⓐⓗN-Yⓐⓗ

cheap (m) رخيص   RO-KHEES

cheap (f) رخيصة   RO-KHEE-Sah

check (restaurant bill) الفاتورة   Fah-TOO-Rah

cheers! الهتافات   FEE SOH-HO-TahK

cheese جبنة   GOB-Nah

chicken فراخ   FRahKH

child (m) طفل   TO-FL

child (f) طفلة   TO-FLah

chocolate شوكولاته   SHO-KO-Lah-Tah

church كنيسة   KO-NEE-Sah

cigar سيجار   SO-GahB

cigarette سيجارة   SO-Gah-Bah

city مدينة   Mah-DEE-Nah

clean (m) نضيف   NEE-DEEF

clean (f) نضيفة   NEE-DEE-Fah

closed (m) مقفول   Mah-FooL

closed (f) مقفولة   Mah-Foo-Lah

clothes هدوم   Hou-DooM

coffee قهوة   'ahH-Wah

cold (m) (temperature) بارد   Bah̄R-OD

cold (f) (temperature) باردة   Bah̄B-Dah

comb مشط   MOSHT

company شركة   SHOB-Kah

computer   كمبيوتر   KOM-BYOO-TahR

conference   مؤتمر   MOU-Tah-MahB

congratulations   مبروك   MahB-BooK

corn   درة   DOO-Bah

crab   كابوريا   Kah-BOB-Yah

cream   قشطة   KBahM

credit card   كريديت كارد   KBeh-DoT KahBT

cup   فنجان   FoN-GahN

customs   الجمارك   oG-Gah-Mah-BoK

D

dangerous (m)   خطير   KHah-TeeR

dangerous (f)   خطيرة   KHah-Tee-Bah

date (calendar)   تاريخ   Tah-BeeKH

day   يوم   YOM

December   ديسمبر   Do-SoM-BoB

delicious (m)   لذيذ   Lah-ZeeZ

delicious (f)   لذيذة   Lah-Zee-Zah

dentist   دكتور الأسنان   DOK-TooB ·ah-SNahN

deodorant   مزيل عرق   MOO-ZeL (ah-Bah·

departure   مغادرة   Sah-FahB

desert (landscape)   الصحرا   Sah-Hah-Bah

dessert (food)   حلويات   Hah-Lah-Wo-YahT

detour لفة TⓐH-WⓔⒺ-Lⓐ

diabetic مريض بالسكر Mⓐ-BⓔⒺD BⓞS-SⓞⓤK-KⓐⒷ

dictionary قاموس Kⓐ-MⓞⓞS

dinner عشا (ⓐ)SH-ⓐⓗ

dining room اودة الاكل Ⓞ-DⓘT ⓘL-·ⓐKL

direction إتّجاه ·ⓘT-Tⓘ-GⓐH

dirty موسخ / موسخة MWⓐ-SⓐKⓗ / MⓘSH Nⓐ-DⒺF

disabled (m) معاق Mⓞ-(ⓐⓗ)K

disabled (f) معاقة Mⓞ-(ⓐⓗ)K-ⓐⓗ

discount تخفيض TⓐKⓗ-FⒺD

distance مسافة Mⓐ-Sⓔ-Fⓐⓗ

doctor (m) دكتور DⓞⓤK-TⓞR

doctor (f) دكتورة DⓞⓤK-Tⓞ-Rⓐⓗ

document وثيقة Wⓐⓗ-SⒺⒺ-Kⓐⓗ

dollar دولار DⓞⓞL-ⓐⓗR (singular) / DⓞⓞL-ⓐⓗ-RⓐⓗT (plural)

down تحت TⓐⓗⒽT

drugstore صيدلية Sⓘ-DⓐⓗL-Lⓘ·-Yⓐⓗ

dry cleaner مغسلة MⓐGH-Sⓐ-Lⓐⓗ

duck بطّة Bⓐⓗ-Tⓐⓗ

E

ear ودن Wⓘ-DⓐN

early بدري BⓐD-BⒺⒺ

east الشرق SH®B

easy (m) سهل S@-HL

easy (f) سهلة S@-HL@

eggs بيض B@D

Egypt مصر M@SB

Egyptian (m) مصري M@S-B®

Egyptian (f) مصرية M@S-B①@

electricity كهربة K@H-B@-B@

elevator اسانسير @-S@N-S®B

embassy سفارة S®-F@-B@

England إنجلترا BB①-T@N-Y@ / ①N-G①L-T®-B@

English (m) إنجليزي ①N-GL®-Z®

English (f) إنجليزية ①N-GL®-Z①@

enough! كفاية K①-F@-Y@

entrance مدخل M@D-KH@L

envelope ظرف Z@BF

everything كل حاجة K@L H@-G@

excellent ممتاز / ممتازة M@M-T@Z / M@M-T@-Z@

exit مخرج M@K-B@G

expensive (m) غالي GH@-L®

expensive (f) غالية GH@-L①@

eye عين @N

F

face وش WⓘSH

far (m) بعيد Bⓘ-(ⒺD

far (f) بعيدة Bⓘ-(Ⓔ-Dⓐⓗ

fare أجرة 'ⓄG-Rⓐⓗ

fast (m) سريع Sⓐⓗ-Rⓔ)

fast (f) سريعة Sⓐⓗ-Rⓔ-(ⓐⓗ

father أبّ 'ⓐⓗB

fax, fax machine فاكس Fⓐ̈KS

February فبراير FⓘB-Rⓐⓗ-YⓘB

few قليل SHWⓘ-Yⓐ̈

finger صباع SⓄ-Bⓐⓗ)

fire! (emergency) نار Hⓐ̈-Rⓔ-'ⓐ̈

fish سمك Sⓐ̈-Mⓐ̈K

flight رحلة Rⓔ̈H-Lⓐⓗ

florist shop محل ورد Mⓐ̈-Hⓐ̈L Wⓐ̈RD

flowers ورد Wⓐ̈R-Dⓐⓗ

food اكل ⓐ̈KL

foot رجل RⓘGL

fork شوكة SHⓄ-Kⓐⓗ

fresh طازة Tⓐⓗ-Zⓐⓗ

Friday الجمعة ⓘL-GⓄ́-Mⓐ(ⓐⓗ

fried (m) مقلى Mֵȃ'-LĒ

fried (f) مقلية Mȃ'-LȊ֍

friend (m) صاحب S֍-ḦȊB

friend (f) صاحبة SȃḦ-B֍

fruit فاكهة Fȃ̂K-Ḧ֍

funny (m) مضحك MֶＯD-ḦȊK

funny (f) مضحكة MֶＯD-ḦȊ-K֍

G

gas بنزين Bȃ̂N-ZĒ̂N

gas station بنزينة Bȃ̂N-ZĒ-N֍

gate بوّابة Bȃ'-Wȃ-B֍

gift هدية HȊ-DȊ'-Yȃ

girl بنت BȊNT

glass (drinking) كاس Kȃ̂S

glasses (eye) نضارة N֍-D֍-B֍

gloves جوانتي GWȃ̂N-TĒ

gold دهب Dֵ̂Ｏ'-Ḧȃ̂B

golf جولف GＯLF

golf course ملعب جولف Mȃ̂L-(ȃ̂B GＯLF

good (m) كويس KWȊ'-YȊS

good (f) كويسة KWȊ'-YȊ-S֍

good-bye مع السلامة M֍-(ȃ̂S-S֍-Lֵ'-M֍

goose وزة   WⓤZ

grape عنب   ①-NⓐP

grateful (m) ممتن   MⓞⓞM-TⓔN

grateful (f) ممتنة   MⓞⓞM-TⓔN-Nⓐh

gray (m) رمادي   Bⓐ-Mⓐh-DEE

gray (f) رمادي   Bⓐ-Mⓐh-D①ⓐh

green (m) اخضر   ⓐKH-Dⓐh-B

green (f) خضرة   KHⓐh-D-Bⓐh

grocery store بقال   Bⓐ-ⓐL

group مجموعة   MⓐG-Mⓞⓞ-ⓐh

guide دليل   Dⓐ-LⓔL

H

hair شعر   SHⓐB

hairbrush فرشة شعر   FⓤB-SH①T SHⓐB

haircut حلقة   HⓐL-ⓐ

ham خنزير   KHⓐN-ZⓔB

hamburger هامبرجر   HⓐM-BⓞⓞB-Gⓐh B

hand ايد   ⓔD

happy (m) مبسوط   Mⓐh B-SⓞⓞT

happy (f) مبسوطة   Mⓐh B-Sⓞⓞ-Tⓐh

he هوه   Hⓞⓦ-Wⓐh

head راس   Bⓐh S

headache صداع   Sⓞⓤ-Dⓐh

health club (gym) جيم   JⒾM

heart condition مشاكل في القلب
 MⒶ-SHⒶ-KⒾL FⒾL-ⒶLB

heart قلب ،ⒶLB

heat حرارة   HⒶ-RⒶ-RⒶh

hello (telephone greeting) الو   ⒶLŌ

help! (cry for help!) الحقوني   ⒶL-HⒶ-Ⓐ-NⒺⒺ

holiday اجازة   Ⓐ-GⒶ-ZⒶ

hospital مستشفى   MⓌS-TⒶSH-FⒶh

hotel فندق   FⓄN-DⓄ،

hour ساعة   SⒺ-Ⓐ

how ازاي   ⒾZ-ZⒶ

hurry up! بسرعة   BⓌ-SⓄ-RⒶh

husband جوز   GⓄⓄZ

I

I انا   Ⓐ-NⒶh

ice تلج   TⒶLG

ice cream ايس كريم   ⒾS KRⒶM

ice cubes مكعبات تلج   MⒾ-KⒶ-،-Ⓐ-BⒶT TⒶLG

ill (m) مريض   MⒶh-RⒺⒺD

ill (f) مريضة   MⒶh-RⒺⒺ-DⒶh

important (m) مهم   MⓌ-HⒾM

important (f) مهمة   MⓌ-HⒾ-MⓌh

indigestion   عسرهضم   ⓞS-BHⓐH-DⓤⓜM

information   استعلامات   Mⓐ)-Lⓞⓞ-MⓐT

interpreter (m)   مترجم   Mⓞⓤ-TⓐB-GⓘM

interpreter (f)   مترجمة   Mⓞⓤ-TⓐB-GⓘM-Mⓐh

Iran   إيران   ⒺⒺ-RⓐⓗN

Iranian (m)   إيراني   ⒺⒺ-Rⓐh-NⒺⒺ

Iranian (f)   إيرانية   ⒺⒺ-Rⓐh-Nⓘⓐh

Iraq   العراق   ⓐL-(ⓘ-Rⓐ∙

Iraqi (m)   عراقي   (ⓘ-Rⓐ∙-∙Ⓔ

Iraqi (f)   عراقية   (ⓘ-Rⓐ∙-∙Ⓘⓐh

Islam   الإسلام   ⓐL-∙ⓘS-LⓐM

Israel   إسرائيل   ⓘS-Rⓐh-∙ⒺL

Israeli (m)   إسرائيلي   ⓘS-Rⓐh-∙Ⓔ-LⒺ

Israeli (f)   إسرائيلية   ⓘS-Rⓐh-∙Ⓔ-Lⓘⓐh

J

jacket   جاكت   Jⓐ-Kⓔ-Tⓐh

jam   مربّى   Mⓐh-Rⓐh-Bⓐh

January   يناير   Yⓐ-Nⓐ-Yⓞ̃R

Jerusalem   القدس   ⓐL-∙ⓞDS

jewelry   مجوهرات   Mⓞⓞ-Gⓞⓦ-Hⓐh-Bⓐh̃T

jewelry store   جواهرجي   Gⓐh-Wⓐh-HⓐB-GⒺ

job   وظيفة   Wⓐh-ZⒺ-Fⓐh

Jordan   الأردن   ⓐL-ʾⓄB-DⓄN

Jordanian (m)   أردني   ⓄB-DⓄ-Nⓔ

Jordanian (f)   أردنية   ⓄB-DⓄ-NⓘⓐH

juice   عصير   ⓐH-SⓔⓔB

July   يولية   YⓞⓞL-Yⓞⓞ

June   يونية   YⓞⓞN-Yⓞⓞ

K

ketchup   كاتشاب   KⓐaT-CHⓘP

key   مفتاح   MⓞⓞF-Tⓐ̈H

kiss   بوسة   Bⓞⓤ-SⓐH

knife   سكينة   SⓘK-Kⓔⓔ-NⓐH

Kuwait   كويت   KⓄ-WⓐT

Kuwaiti (m)   كويتي   KⓄ-Wⓐ-Tⓔⓔ

Kuwaiti (f)   كويتية   KⓄ-Wⓐ-TⓘⓐH

L

ladies' room   حمام السيدات   Hⓐ̈M-Mⓐ̈M   ⓘ-SⓘT-TⓄT

ladies   السيدات   ⓘS-ⓐH-Yⓔ̈-DⓐHT

lamb   ضاني   DⓐH-Nⓔⓔ

language   لغة   Lⓞⓤ-GHⓐ̈

large (m)   كبير   KⓘB-Bⓔ̈B

large (f)   كبيرة   KⓘB-Bⓔⓔ-BⓐH

late (m)   متأخر   MⓘT-ʾⓐHKHⓗ-ⓐHB

late (f)   متأخرة   MⓄT-•ⓐⓀ-ⓐh-Ⓑⓐh

laundry   مغسلة   MⓐGH-SⓐⒽ-Ⓛⓐh

lawyer (m)   محامي   MⓄ-HⓐⒽ-Mⓔⓔ

lawyer (f)   محامية   MⓄ-HⓐⒽ-Mⓔⓔⓦh

Lebanon   لبنان   LⓄ́B-Nⓐ́N

Lebanese (m)   لبناني   LⓄ́B-Nⓐ-Nⓔⓔ

Lebanese (f)   لبنانية   LⓄ́B-Nⓐ-Nⓔⓔ-Yⓐh

left (direction)   شمال   SHⓄ-Mⓐ́L

leg   رجل   BⓄGL

lemon   لمون   Lⓐ̌-MⓄⓄN

less   أقل   ⓐ-•ⓐ́L

letter   جواب   Gⓐh-Wⓐ̌B

lettuce   خسّ   KHⓐⓢS

Libya   ليبيا   LⓄ́B-Yⓐ̌

Libyan (m)   ليبي   Lⓔⓔ́-Bⓔⓔ

Libyan (f)   ليبية   Lⓔⓔ-Bⓔⓔ́-Ⓤh

light   نور   NⓄⓄB

lips   شفايف   SHⓐ̌-Fⓐ̌-YⓄF

lipstick   روج   BⓄⓄZH

little (m) (amount)   قليل   Ⓞⓤ̌-LⓄ-YⓄL

little (f) (amount)   قليلة   Ⓞⓤ̌-LⓄ-YⓄ́-Lⓐh

little (m) (size)   صغير   SⓄ-GHⓐȟ-YⓐhB

little (f) (size)   صغيرة   SⓄ-GHⓐȟ-YⓐhB-ⓐh

lobster استاكوزا ⓔS-Tⓐ-Kⓞⓞ-Zⓐⓗ

long (m) طويل Tⓐⓗ-WⓔⓔL

long (f) طويلة Tⓐⓗ-Wⓔⓔ-Lⓐⓗ

lost (m) تايه Tⓐ-Y①H

lost (f) تايهة T①-Hⓐⓗ

luck حظّ HⓐⓗZ

luggage شنط SHⓞ-NⓐⓗT

lunch غدا GHⓐ-Dⓐⓗ

M

maid خدامة KⓗⓐⓗD-Dⓔ-Mⓐⓗ

mail بريد Bⓐ-RⓔⓔD

makeup مكياج M①K-YⓐZH

man راجل Bⓐⓗ-G①L

map خريطة KHⓐⓗ-Rⓔⓔ-Tⓐⓗ

March مارس Mⓐ-R①S

market سوق Sⓞⓞ'

matches (cigarette) كبريت KⓐB-RⓔⓔT

May مايو M①-Yⓞⓞ

mayonnaise مايونيز M①-Y①-NⓐZ

meal وجبة WⓐⓗG-Bⓐⓗ

meat لحمة LⓐⓗH-Mⓐ

mechanic ميكانيكي Mⓐ-Kⓐ-Nⓔⓔ-Kⓔⓔ

meeting إجتماع ①G-T①-Mⓐ

mens' restroom حمام الرجال
  HⓐM-MⓐM ①B-Ⓡ①-Gⓐ-Lⓐ

menu منيو MⒺN-Y⊚⊚

message رسالة RⒺ-Sⓐ-Lⓐ

Middle East الشرق الأوسط Ⓔ-SHⓐRⓀ ⒺL-·⊙Ⓦ-SⓐⓗT

milk لبن Lⓐ-BⓐN

mineral water مية معدنية M①-Yⓐⓗ Mⓐⓗ-DⒺ-N①-Yⓐⓗ

minute دقيقة D①-·ⒺⒺ-·ⓐ

Miss آنسة ⓐ-NⒺ-Sⓐⓗ

mistake غلط GHⓐⓗ-LⓐⓗT

misunderstanding سوء فهم S⊚⊚· Tⓐ-Fⓐ-HⓄM

moment لحظة Lⓐⓗ-Hⓐⓗ-Zⓐⓗ

Monday الإتنين ①L-L①T-NⓐN

money فلوس FL⊚⊚S

month شهر SHⓐⓗHⓇ

monument نصب N⊙-S⊙B

more اكتر ⓐⓗK-TⓐⓗR

morning الصبح Ⓔ-S⊙PH

mosque مسجد MⒺS-G①D

mother أم ⓄM

mountain جبل Gⓐ-BⓐL

movies السينما S①-NⒺ-Mⓐⓗ

Mr. السّيد ⓐS-S①-ⒺⒺD

Mrs. السّيدة ⓐS-S①-YⒺ-Dⓐⓗ

much كثير KⒾ-TⒺⒺR

museum متحف MⓐT-ⒽⓐF

mushrooms عش الغراب ⒶSH ⒾL-GHⓄ-RⓐB

music موسيقى Mⓞⓞ-SⒺⒺ-Kⓐ

mustard مسطردة MⓄS-TⓐR-Dⓐ

N

name اسم ⒾSM

napkin منديل MⓐN-DⒺⒺL

near (m) قريب ‘Ⓞ-BⒾ-YⒺB

near (f) قريبة ‘Ⓞ-RⒺⒺ-Yⓐ-Bⓐ

neck رقبة Rⓐ-‘ⓐ-Bⓐ

never أبدا ⓐ-Bⓐ-DⓐN

newspaper الجرنال GⓞⓞR-NⓐL

news stand بياع الجرايد BⒾ-ⓐ ⒾL-Gⓐ-Rⓐ-YⓐD

night بالليل BⒾL-LⓐL

nightclub نايت كلوب NⒾT-KLⓄⓤB

no لا Lⓐ‘

noon الضهر Ⓘ-DⓄHR

north الشمال SHⓐ-MⓐL

notary كاتب Kⓐ-TⒾB

November نوفمبر Nⓞⓤ-VⒾM-BⒾR

now دلوقتي DⒾL-Wⓐ‘-TⒺⒺ

number رقم Rⓐⓐ-KⓐM

nurse ممرضة M@@-M@h-R①-D@h

O

occupied (m) مشغول M@SH-GH@@L

occupied (f) مشغولة M@SH-GH@@L-@h

ocean محيط M@-H①T

October أكتوبر @K-T@-B@B

officer ظابط Z@h-B@T

oil زيت Z@T

omelet بيض مقلي B@D @M-L①T

one-way (traffic) اتجاه واحد ①-T①-G@H W@-H①D

onion بصل B@h-S@L

open مفتوح M@hF-T@@H

opera الأوبرا @-B@-B@h

operator مشغل M@@-SH@-GH@L

orange (color) برتقاني B@B-T@@-·@h-N@@

owner مالك M@-L①K

oysters محار M@h-H@hB

P

package علبة @L-B@h

paid (m) مدفوع M@D-F@@·

paid (f) مدفوعة M@D-F@@-·@h

pain ألم @-L@hM

painting صورة S◌̅◌̅-Rⓐ

Palestine فلسطين Fⓘ-Lⓘ̇S-Tⓔ̈N

Palestinian (m) فلسطيني Fⓘ-Lⓘ̇S-Tⓔ̈-Nⓔ

Palestinian (f) فلسطينية Fⓘ-Lⓘ̇S-Tⓔ̈-Nⓐ-ⓤ

paper ورقة Wⓐ-Rⓐ-ʼⓐ

partner (business) شريك / شريكة SHⓘ-Rⓔ̈K

party حفلة Hⓐ̈F-Lⓐ

passenger (m) مسافر M◌̅◌̅-Sⓐ̈-Fⓘ̇R

passenger (f) مسافرة M◌̅◌̅-Sⓐ̈-Fⓘ̇R-ⓐ

passport باسبور Gⓐ-Wⓐ̈Z Sⓐ-Fⓘ̇R

pasta مكرونة Mⓐ-Kⓐ-Rⓞ̇-Nⓐ

pastry عجاين ⓐ-Gⓐ̈-Yⓘ̇N

pen قلم جاف ⓐ̈-Lⓐ̈M Gⓐ̈F

pencil قلم رصاص ⓐ̈-Lⓐ̈M Rⓞ-Sⓐ̈S

pepper فلفل Fⓘ̇L-Fⓘ̇L

perfume برفان Bⓐ̈R-Fⓐ̈N

person شخص SHⓐ̈KⓔS

pharmacist صيدلي Sⓘ̇-Dⓐ̈-Lⓔ̈

pharmacy صيدلية Sⓘ̇-Dⓐ̈-Lⓘ̇-Yⓐ

phone book اجندة التليفون
  ⓐ̈-Gⓘ̇N-Dⓘ̇T ⓘ̇-Tⓔ-Lⓔ-Fⓘ̇N

photo صورة S◌̅◌̅-Rⓐ

photographer مصور M◌̅◌̅-Sⓐ̈-Wⓘ̇R

pillow مخدة   M㏒-KⒽⒶD-Dⓐh

pink (m) وردي   WⓐR̓B-DⒺⒺ

pink (f) وردية   WⓐR̓B-DⒶ-Yⓐh

pizza بتزا   BⒾD-Zⓐh

plastic بلاستك   BLⒺ̓S-TⓄK

plate طبق   Tⓐh-Bⓐh·

please (m) من فضلك   MⒾN FⓐD̓D-LⓐK

please (f) من فضلك   MⒾN FⓐD̓D-LⒾK

pleasure متعة   MⓄ-Tⓐh

police الشرطة / البوليس   BⓄ-LⒺⒺS / SHⓄR̓B-Tⓜ

police station القسم   ⒾL-·ⒾSM

pork خنزير   KⒽⒶN-ZⒺⒺR

porter شيّال   SHⒶ̓-YⓄL

post office بوسطة   BⓄ̓S-Tⓐh

postcard كارت معايدة   KⓐRT MⓄ-Ⓒ̓-Dⓐh

potatoes بطاطس   Bⓐh-Tⓐh-TⒾS

pregnant حامل   ĤⒶ̃-MⒾL

prescription روشتة   B㏒-SHⒶ̓T-Tⓐh

price تمن   TⒶ̃-MⒶN

problem مشكلة   M㏒SH-KⒺ̓-Lⓐh

profession مهنة   MⒶ̓H-Nⓐh

public telephone تليفون عمومي
    TⒺ-LⒺⒺ-FⓄ̓N (Ⓞ-M㏒-MⒺⒺ

purified صافي   S@-F©

purple (m) أرجواني   @B-G@-W@-N©

purple (f) أرجوانية   @B-G@-W@-N@-Y@

purse (small purse / bag) شنطة / بوك
 B@K / SH@N-T@

Q

quality جودة   G@-D@

question سؤال   S@-·@L

quickly بسرعة   B@-S@B-·@

R

radio راديو   B@D-Y@

rain مطر   M@-T@B

raincoat سويتر   SW©-T@B

ramp مطلعاية   M@T-L@-@-Y@

razor blade مكنة حلاقة   M@-K@-N@T H©-L@-·@

ready (m) جاهز   G@-H@Z

ready (f) جاهزة   G@H-Z@

receipt وصل   W@SL

red (m) أحمر   @H-M@B

red (f) حمرة   H@M-B@

repeat! (To a man) عيد   (©D

repeat! (To a woman) عيدي   (©-D©

restaurant   مطعم   M@-T@M

rice (cooked)   رز   B⊚Z

rich (m)   غني   GH@-N⒠

rich (f)   غنية   GH@-N⒠-Y@

right (correct)   صح   S@H̱

right (direction)   يمين   Y⒠-M⒠N

river   نهر   N@H̱R

road   طريق   T@-R⒠

room   اودة   (⊙-D@)

S

safe (hotel)   خزنة   KH@Z-N@

salad   سلطة   S@-L@-T@

sale   اوكازيون   ⊙-K@Z-Y⊚N

salmon   سلامون   S@-L@-M⊙N

salt   ملح   M@LH̱

sandwich   سندويتش   S@ND-W⒤CH

Saturday   السّبت   ⒤S-S@BT

scissors   مقص   M@-@S

Saudi Arabia   السعودية   @-S@-⊚-D@-Y@

Saudian (m)   سعودي   S@-⊚-D⒠

Saudian (f)   سعودية   S@-⊚-D⒠-Y@

seafood   اطعمة بحرية   @-T⒤-M@ B@-H̱@-R⒤-Y@

season   فصل   F@SL

seat كرسي K@B-S@

secretary (m) سكرتير S@-K①B-T@B

secretary (f) سكرتيرة S@-K①B-T@-B@

section قسم K①SM

September سبتمبر S@B-T@M-B①B

service خدمة K①D-M@

several (m) مختلف M@K①-T@-L①F

several (f) مختلفة M@K①-T@-L①-F@

shampoo شامبو SH@M-B@

sheets (bed) ملايات M①-L①-@T

shirt قميص @-M@S

shoes جزمة G@Z-M@

shoe store محل الجزم M@-H@L ①-G@-Z@M

shopping center مول M@L

shower دش D@SH

shrimp جمبري G@M-B@-B@

sick (m) مريض M@-B@D

sick (f) مريضة M@-B@-D@

sign (display) علامة (@-L@-M@

signature توقيع ①M-D@

silence! هدوء H@-D@

single (unmarried) (m) عازب (@-Z①B

single (unmarried) (f) عازية (@Z-B@

sir السيد ⓐS-S①-①D

sister أخت ⓞⓚⓢT

size مقاس Mⓐ-ⓐS

skin بشرة Bⓐ̓SH-Bⓐ̔

skirt جيبة Jⓔⓔ-Bⓐ̔

sky السما، ①S-Sⓐ-Mⓐ̔

sleeve كمّ KⓞⓞM

slowly ببطئ B①-B⃝̓T،

small (m) صغير Sⓞ-GH①̓-Yⓐ̔R

small (f) صغيرة Sⓞ-GH①̓-Yⓐ̔-Rⓐ̔

soap صابون Sⓐ̔-BⓞⓞN

socks شرابات SHⓐ̔R-Bⓐ̔T

some بعض Bⓐ̔D

something حاجة Hⓐ-Gⓐ̔

sometimes احيانا ⓐ̓H-Yⓐ-Nⓐ̓N

soon قريب، ⓞ-Bⓐ̔-Y①B

sorry (I am) أسف ⓐS-S①F

soup شورية SHⓞ̓B-Bⓐ̔

south الجنوب ⓔL-Gⓐ-NⓞⓞB

souvenir تذكار Tⓐ̔Z-Kⓐ̔B-ⓐ̔

Spain اسبانيا ⓐS-Bⓐ̓N-①ⓐ̔

Spaniard (m) اسباني ⓐS-Bⓐ̓-Nⓔⓔ

Spaniard (f) اسبانية ⓐS-Bⓐ̓-Nⓐ-Yⓐ̔

specialty التخصص T@h-K@h-S@S

speed السرعة S@B-@h

spoon معلقة M@h-L@-'@h

sport رياضة B@-Y@h-D@h

spring (season) الربيع (@B-B@h-B@)

stairs سلالم S@-L@-L@M

stamp طابع T@h-B@

station (train) محطة M@h-H@h-T@T @L @TB

steak ستيك ST@K

steamed مطبوخ علي البخار B@L-B@-K@h-B

stop! اقف @-'@F

store مخزن M@h-H@L

storm عاصفة (@h-S@-F@h)

straight ahead علاطول (@h-L@h-T@L)

strawberry فراولة F@h-B@-L@h

street شارع SH@-B@

string خيط K@T

subway مترو M@-TB@

Sudan سودان @S-S@-D@N

Sudanese (m) سوداني S@-D@-N@

Sudanese (f) سودانية S@-D@-N@-Y@h

sugar سكّر S@-K@B

suit (clothes) بدلة B@D-L@h

suitcase شنطة سفر SH@N-T①T S@-F@B

summer الصيف ①S-S@F

sun شمس SH@MS

suntan lotion صن تان Z@T S@N-T@N

Sunday الحد ①L-H@D

sunglasses نضارة شمس N@-D@-B①T SH@MS

supermarket سوبر ماركت S@-B@B M@B-K①T

surprise مفاجأة M@-F@G-•@

sweet (m) مسكر M①-S@K-@B

sweet (f) مسكرة M①-S@K-@-B@

swimming pool حمام سباحة H@M-M@M S@-B@-H@

synagogue معبد M@)-B@D

T

table ترابيزة T@-B@-B@Z-@

tampon فوط صحية F①-T@ S①H-H①@

tape (sticky) لزق L@-Z•

tape recorder شريط SH@-B@T

tax ضرايب D@-B@-Y①B

taxi تاكسي T@K-S@

tea شاي SH@-@

telephone تليفون T@-L@-F@N

television تلفزيون T@-L@-V①Z-Y@N

tennis تنس T@-N①S

tennis court ملعب تنس   MⓐL-(ⓐB TⒺ-NⓘS

thank you! شكرا   SHⓄⓊK-Rⓐ\N

that ده   Dⓐh

theater (movie) السينما   SⓘN-Ⓔ-Mⓐh

there همه   HⓄ-Mⓐh

they همه   HⓄ-Mⓐh

this ده   Dⓐh

thread (sewing) غرزة   GHⓄR-Zⓐh

throat زور   ZⓄR

Thursday الخميس   ⓐL-KHⓐh-MⒺS

ticket تذكرة   TⓐZ-Kⓐh-Rⓐh

tie كرافتة   Kⓐh-Rⓐh-Vⓐh-Tⓐh

time وقت   Wⓐ·T

tip (gratuity) بقشيش   Bⓐ·-SHⒺSH

tire عجلة   (ⓐ-Gⓐ-Lⓐh

toast (bread) توست   TⓄST

tobacco تبغ   TⓐGH

today النهاردة   ⓘ-Nⓐh-Hⓐh\R-Dⓐh

toe صباع الرجل   SⓄ-Bⓐ) ⓘR-RⓘGL

together مع بعض   Mⓐ)-Bⓐh)D

toilet التواليت   TWⓐh-LⓘT

toilet paper ورق تواليت   Wⓐ-Rⓐh· TWⓐh-LⓘT

tomato طماطم   Tⓐh-Mⓐ-TⓘM

tomorrow　بكرة　BOK-Bah

toothache　وجع أسنان　Wah-G-ah) ·ah-S-NahN

toothbrush　فرشة أسنان　FOOB-SHOT · ah-S-NahN

toothpaste　معجون أسنان　Mah)-GOON · ah-S-NahN

toothpick　خلة سنان　KHOL-LOT · ah-S-NahN

tour　جولة　GOW-Lah

tourist (m)　سايح　SA-YOH

tourist (f)　سايحة　SA-YHah

tourist office　مكتب سياحة
MAK-TahB SA-Fah-BO-YahT

towel　فوطة　FO-Tah

train　قطر　ah-TB

traveler's check　شيكات سفر　SHEE-KahT Sah-FahB

trip　رحلة　BOH-Lah

truth　حقيقة　Hah-·EE-·ah

Tuesday　التلات　OT-Tah-LahT

Tunisia　تونس　TOO-NOS

Tunisian (m)　تونسي　TOO-NOO-SEE

Tunisian (f)　تونسية　TOO-NOO-SA-Yah

Turkey　تركيا　TOOB-KO-Yah

Turkish (m)　تركي　TOOB-KEE

Turkish (f)　تركية　TOOB-KA-Yah

turkey　ديك رومى　DEEK BOO-MEE

U

umbrella شمسية SH@M-S①-Y@

underwear ملابس داخلية
M@-L@-P①S D@-K①-L①-@

United Kingdom بريطانيا BR①-T@N-Y@

United States امريكا @M-R@-K@

university جامعة G@M-(@

up فوق F@'

urgent (m) مستعجل M①S-T@-G①L

urgent (f) مستعجلة M①S-T@-G①-L@

V

vacant (m) فاضي F@-D@

vacant (f) فاضية F@-D①-@

vacation اجازة @-G@-Z@

valuable قيم K@-Y①M

value قيمة K@-M@

vanilla (flavor) فانيليا V@-N①L-Y@

veal بتلو B①-T①L-L@

vegetables خضار K①-D@R

view منظر M@N-Z@R

vinegar خلّ K@L

W

wait! استنه   ①S-TⓐN-Nⓐh

waiter جارسون   GⓐB-SⓞN

waitress جارسونة   GⓐB-Sⓞ-Nⓐh

watch out! (m) خلى بالك   K⒣ⓐ-L⒠⒠ Bⓐ-LⓐK

watch out! (f) خلى بالك   K⒣ⓐ-L⒠⒠ Bⓐ-L①K

water مية   M①-Yⓐh

watermelon بطيخ   Bⓐ-T⒠⒠-K⒣

we احنه   ⒠H-Nⓐh

weather الجو   ①L-Gⓞⱳ

Wednesday الأربع   ①L (ⓐB-Bⓐh)

week اسبوع   ①S-B⓪)

weekend أخر الاسبوع   ⓐh-K⒣①B ①L ·①S-B⓪)

welcome اهلا   ·ⓐh-LⓐN

well done (cooked) مستوي   M⒠S-T①-W⒠⒠

west الغرب   ①L GHⓐRB

wheelchair كرسي بعجل   K⓪B-S⒠⒠ B①-(ⓐh-GⓐL

when? إمته؟   ⓐM-Tⓐh

where? فين؟   FⓐN

which? أنهي؟   ⓐN-H⒠⒠

white (m) أبيض   ⓐB-YⓐD

white (f) بيضة   Bⓐ-Dⓐh

who? مين؟ MⒺN

why? ليه؟ LⒶ

wife زوجة ZⓄ-Gⓐ

wind ريح BⒺH

window شباك SHⓄB-BⓐK

wine نبيت NⓄ-BⒺT

winter الشتا ⓄSH-SHⓄ-Tⓐ

with مع Mⓐ-ⓐ

woman ست SⓄT

wonderful (m) رائع Bⓐ-Ⓞ)

wonderful (f) رائعة Bⓐ-Ⓞ-(ⓐ

world عالم (Ⓞ-Lⓐ)M

wrong غلط GHⓐ-LⓐT

XYZ

year سنة Sⓐ-Nⓐ

yellow (m) أصفر ⓐS-FⓐR

yellow (f) صفره SⓐF-Bⓐ

yes ايوة Ⓞ-Wⓐ

yesterday إمبارح ⓐM-Bⓐ-BⓄH

you إنته ⓐN-Tⓐ

zipper سوستة SⓄⓊS-Tⓐ

zoo جنينة الحيوانات
GⓄ-NⓄ-NⓄT ⓐL HⓄ-Yⓐ-Wⓐ-NⓐT

THANKS!

The nicest thing you can say to anyone in any language is "Thank you." Try some of these languages using the incredible Vowel Symbol System.

Spanish	**French**
GRah-SEE-ahS	MÕR-SEE
German	**Italian**
DahN-Kuh	GRahT-SEE-ẽ
Japanese	**Chinese**
DO-MO	SHEEẽ SHEEẽ

Swedish	Portuguese
T@hK	@-BR(EE)-G@h-D@

Arabic	Greek
SH(oo)-KR@hN	(ĕ)F-H@h-R(EE)-ST@́

Hebrew	Russian
T@-D@h́	SP@h-S(EE)́-B@h

Swahili	Dutch
@h-S@hN-T@	D@hNK (oo)

Tagalog	Hawaiian
S@h-L@h-M@h́T	M@h-H@h-L@

INDEX

CPSIA information can be obtained
at www.ICGtesting.com
Printed in the USA
LVHW080501300122
709678LV00014B/456

9 780071 544580